IGCSE Mathematics Practice

for Edexcel
Second Edition

TREVOR JOHNSON
TONY CLOUGH

Acknowledgements

This material has been endorsed by Edexcel and offers high quality support for the delivery of Edexcel qualifications.

Edexcel endorsement does not mean that this material is essential to achieve any Edexcel qualification, nor does it mean that this is the only suitable material available to support any Edexel qualification. No endorsed material will be used verbatim in setting any Edexcel examination and any resource lists produced by Edexcel shall include this and other appropriate texts. While this material has been through an Edexcel quality assurance process, all responsibility for the content remains with the publisher.

Copies of official specifications for all Edexcel qualifications may be found on the Edexcel website – www.edexcel.com

Every effort has been made to trace all copyright holders, but if any have been inadvertently overlooked the publishers will be pleased to make the necessary arrangements at the first opportunity.

Although every effort has been made to ensure that website addresses are correct at time of going to press, Hodder Education cannot be held responsible for the content of any website mentioned in this book. It is sometimes possible to find a relocated web page by typing in the address of the home page for a website in the URL window of your browser.

Hachette's policy is to use papers that are natural, renewable and recyclable products and made from wood grown in sustainable forests. The logging and manufacturing processes are expected to conform to the environmental regulations of the country of origin.

Orders: please contact Bookpoint Ltd, 130 Milton Park, Abingdon, Oxon OX14 4SB. Telephone: (44) 01235 827720. Fax: (44) 01235 400454. Lines are open 9.00 – 5.00, Monday to Saturday, with a 24-hour message answering service. Visit our website at www.hoddereducation.co.uk

© Trevor Johnson, Tony Clough, 2011
First published by
Hodder Education,
an Hachette UK Company
338 Euston Road
London NW1 3BH

This second edition published in 2011

Impression number   5   4
Year   2015   2014   2013

Cover illustration © David Angel @ Début Art
Typeset in 11 point Times Ten Roman by Tech-Set Ltd
Printed in Great Britain by CPI (UK) Ltd, Croydon, CRO 4YY

A catalogue record for this title is available from the British Library

ISBN: 978 1444 138 245

CONTENTS

Introduction   iv

Number

1 Decimals   1
2 Powers and roots   4
3 Fractions   7
4 Percentages   10
5 Ratio and proportion   15
6 Standard form   18
7 Degree of accuracy   23
8 Set language and notation   27

Algebra

9   Algebraic manipulation   31
10 Expressions and formulae   34
11 Linear equations and
    simultaneous equations   37
12 Coordinates and graphs   40
13 Linear graphs   43
14 Integer sequences   48
15 Quadratic equations   50
16 Inequalities   52
17 Indices   56
18 Proportion   58
19 Function notation   61
20 Harder graphs   63
21 Calculus   68

Shape, Space and Measures

22 Average speed   71
23 Construction   73
24 Geometry   75
25 Transformations   79
26 Circle properties   83
27 Area and perimeter   88
28 3-D shapes – volume and surface
    area   92
29 Pythagoras' theorem   97
30 Trigonometry   105
31 Similar shapes   114
32 Advanced trigonometry   120
33 Vectors   126

Handling Data

34 Graphical representation
    of data   130
35 Statistical measures   135
36 Probabilty   143

Answers   152

INTRODUCTION

Written by experienced senior examiners, *IGCSE Mathematics Practice* includes hundreds of exam-type questions. This book will be a valuable additional resource for all schools preparing candidates for Edexcel's IGCSE mathematics and Edexcel Certificate Higher tier papers, regardless of the text books being used in lessons. The sections correspond to those in the scheme of work in the Teacher's Guide, which is available from Edexcel Publications.

As it is envisaged that this book will often be used as part of students' final preparation for the exam, to provide appropriately varied practice covering all the relevant grades, each section contains a variety of questions which are not in any particular order.

There are questions addressing every part of the latest Specification A. The authors have included examples of the new types of questions on fractions, standard form and surds. There are also questions on compound interest and repeated percentage change, which are the only significant additional topics in the revised specifications. For each question, there is an indication of mark tariff it might carry in an exam but this should be regarded only as a guide. Short numerical and algebraic answers are also provided.

The authors would like to thank the staff of Hodder Education for the valuable help and advice they have given.

Trevor Johnson, Tony Clough

Number

1 Decimals

1   Karl has a mobile phone. Last month, he paid 12.8p for each minute of calls plus a monthly charge of £15.25
Last month, Karl made 246 minutes of calls.
Work out the **total** amount that Karl paid last month.

(Total 3 marks)

2   Anna is a freelance typist. She types at a rate of 60 words per minute.
Anna charges 0.4p per word.
a)   Work out how much Anna charges for one hour's typing.   **(2)**

Anna types a document of 14 000 words.
b)   i)   How much will Anna charge for typing the document?
ii)   How long will it take Anna to type the document?   **(5)**

(Total 7 marks)

3   Hassan buys a new car.
The car's petrol tank has a capacity of 58.5 litres.
The cost of petrol is 95.1p per litre, of which 65.7p is tax.
The car can travel 15.2 km on one litre of petrol.
a)   Work out the cost of a full tank of petrol.   **(2)**

Hassan drove 19 200 km last year.
b)   Work out how much tax Hassan paid when driving 19 200 km.
Give your answer to the nearest pound.   **(3)**

(Total 5 marks)

4   Andre used 1521 units of electricity.
The first 207 units cost £0.1708 per unit.
The remaining units cost £0.0943 per unit.
Tax is added at 5% of the total amount.
Complete a copy of Andre's bill.

207 units at £0.1708 per unit	£ ....
...... units at £0.0943 per unit	£ ....
Total amount	£ _____
Tax at 5% of the total amount	£ ....
Amount to pay	£ _____

(Total 7 marks)

5 Work out the value of $\dfrac{17.16}{1.4 + 2.5}$

(Total 2 marks)

6 Work out the value of $\dfrac{7.3 + 9.5}{8.4 - 3.6}$

(Total 2 marks)

7 Use your calculator to work out the value of $\dfrac{8.3 - 2.7}{1.7 \times 0.4}$

Write down all the figures on your calculator display.

(Total 2 marks)

8 a) Use your calculator to work out the value of $\dfrac{8.7 \times 5.24}{8.02 + 1} - 3.6$

Write down all the figures on your calculator display. **(2)**

b) Give your answer to part **a)** correct to 3 significant figures. **(1)**

(Total 3 marks)

9 a) Use your calculator to work out the value of $2.7 - \dfrac{9.7}{1.9 + 1.7}$

Write down all the figures on your calculator display. **(2)**

b) Give your answer to part **a)** correct to 2 significant figures. **(1)**

(Total 3 marks)

10 a) Use your calculator to work out the value of $\dfrac{(12.71 - 3.9)^2}{3.7 + 5.43}$

Write down all the figures on your calculator display. **(2)**

b) Give your answer to part **a)** correct to 2 decimal places. **(1)**

(Total 3 marks)

11 Show that $0.35 + \dfrac{2}{7} = \dfrac{89}{140}$

(Total 3 marks)

12 Prove that the recurring decimal $0.\dot{7} = \dfrac{7}{9}$

(Total 2 marks)

13 Convert the recurring decimal $0.6\dot{3}$ to a fraction.
Give your answer in its simplest form.

(Total 2 marks)

14 x is an integer such that $1 \leqslant x < 10$
y is an integer such that $1 \leqslant y < 10$

Prove that $0.0\dot{x}\dot{y} = \dfrac{xy}{990}$

(Total 2 marks)

15 Prove that the recurring decimal $0.5\dot{3} = \dfrac{8}{15}$

(Total 2 marks)

16 Convert the recurring decimal $0.6\dot{4}$ to a fraction.
Give your answer in its simplest form.

(Total 2 marks)

17 Bhavana says:

'When the fraction $\dfrac{n}{105}$ is converted to a decimal, it never gives a terminating decimal.'

a) Find a value of n less than 105, which shows that Bhavana is wrong.

b) Write down the type of number n must be, when $\dfrac{n}{105}$ gives a terminating decimal.

(Total 2 marks)

2 Powers and roots

1 Calculate the value of $\sqrt{3.7^3 - 4.2^2}$
Write down all the figures on your calculator display.

(Total 2 marks)

2 a) Use your calculator to work out the value of $\sqrt{\dfrac{2.7}{1.2^2 + 0.9}}$

Write down all the figures on your calculator display. **(2)**

b) Give your answer to part **a)** correct to 3 significant figures. **(1)**

(Total 3 marks)

3 a) Use your calculator to work out the value of $\dfrac{\sqrt{4.3 + 2.9^3}}{1.3} + 3.6^2$

Write down all the figures on your calculator display. **(2)**

b) Give your answer to part **a)** correct to 2 decimal places. **(1)**

(Total 3 marks)

4 a) Calculate the value of $\dfrac{(4.6^2 - 1.9^3)}{\sqrt{2.4 + 4.8}}$

Write down all the figures on your calculator display. **(2)**

b) Give your answer to part **a)** correct to 4 significant figures. **(1)**

(Total 3 marks)

5 Express 175 as the product of its prime factors.

(Total 2 marks)

6 Express 392 as a product of powers of its prime factors.

(Total 3 marks)

7 Express 300 as a product of powers of its prime factors.

(Total 3 marks)

8 a) i) Express 108 as a product of powers of its prime factors.
  ii) Express 144 as a product of powers of its prime factors. **(4)**
  b) Using your answers to part **a)**, or otherwise, work out the Highest Common
  Factor of 108 and 144 **(2)**

(Total 6 marks)

9 **a)** Express 150 as the product of its prime factors. (2)
   b) Work out the Lowest Common Multiple of 90 and 150 (2)

(**Total 4 marks**)

10 **a)** Find the Highest Common Factor of 105 and 147 (2)
    b) Find the Lowest Common Multiple of 105 and 147 (2)

(**Total 4 marks**)

11

Symbols
$+$ $-$ $\times$ $\div$ $(\;)$

Using only symbols from the box, make the following into true statements.
a) 6   4   2 $=$ 20 (1)
b) 6   4   2 $=$ 3.5 (1)
c) 6   4   2 $= \frac{3}{4}$ (1)

(**Total 3 marks**)

12 **a)** Find, as a fraction, the value of $\dfrac{4 + 2^3}{(4 + 2)^2}$

    b) Write your answer to part **a)** as a decimal.

(**Total 3 marks**)

13 **a)** Simplify, leaving your answer in index form
      i) $5^4 \times 5^8$ **ii)** $9^7 \div 9^4$ (2)

    b) Solve $\dfrac{3^8 \times 3^5}{3^n} = 3^4$ (2)

(**Total 4 marks**)

14 **a)** Simplify, leaving your answer in index form
      i) $4^7 \times 4$ **ii)** $6^3 \div 6^5$ (2)

    b) $7^y = 1$
      Find the value of y. (1)

(**Total 3 marks**)

15 Evaluate the following.
Give your answers as fractions.

a) 3^{-4} **(1)**

b) $\left(\dfrac{64}{343}\right)^{\frac{1}{3}}$ **(1)**

c) $\left(\dfrac{\sqrt{6}}{4}\right)^4$ **(1)**

(Total 3 marks)

16 a) Express $27^{\frac{1}{2}}$ as a power of 3 **(2)**

b) Express $\sqrt{2}$ as a power of 8 **(2)**

c) Express $\dfrac{\sqrt{2}}{16}$ as a power of 2 **(3)**

(Total 7 marks)

17 Show that $(2 - \sqrt{3})^2 = 7 - 4\sqrt{3}$

(Total 2 marks)

18 Show that $\sqrt{147} = 7\sqrt{3}$

(Total 2 marks)

19 a) Show that $\sqrt{32} - \sqrt{8} = 2\sqrt{2}$ **(2)**

b) Show that $(1 + 2\sqrt{3})^2 = 13 + 4\sqrt{3}$ **(2)**

(Total 4 marks)

20 Show that $\left(\dfrac{1}{\sqrt{2}}\right)^7 = \dfrac{\sqrt{2}}{16}$

(Total 3 marks)

21 a) Show that $(1 - \sqrt{3})^2 = 4 - 2\sqrt{3}$ **(2)**

b) Hence show that $\dfrac{(1 - \sqrt{3})^2}{\sqrt{3}} = -2 + \dfrac{4\sqrt{3}}{3}$ **(3)**

(Total 5 marks)

3 Fractions

1 Show that $\frac{1}{3} + \frac{2}{5} = \frac{11}{15}$

(Total 2 marks)

2 Show that $\frac{4}{15} \times 6 = 1\frac{3}{5}$

(Total 2 marks)

3 Show that $\frac{6}{7} \times \frac{1}{9} = \frac{2}{21}$

(Total 2 marks)

4 Show that $\frac{2}{9} \div \frac{1}{4} = \frac{8}{9}$

(Total 2 marks)

5 Show that $\frac{11}{12} - \frac{2}{3} = \frac{1}{4}$

(Total 2 marks)

6 Show that $\frac{9}{10} \times \frac{2}{3} = \frac{3}{5}$

(Total 2 marks)

7 Show that $\frac{3}{8} \div \frac{5}{12} = \frac{9}{10}$

(Total 2 marks)

8 Show that $\frac{3}{4} + \frac{4}{9} = 1\frac{7}{36}$

(Total 2 marks)

9 Show that $\frac{8}{9} \div 6 = \frac{4}{27}$

(Total 2 marks)

10 Show that $3\frac{2}{9} + 1\frac{5}{6} = 5\frac{1}{18}$

(Total 3 marks)

11 Show that $2\frac{2}{5} \times 1\frac{1}{9} = 2\frac{2}{3}$

(Total 3 marks)

12 Show that $4\frac{3}{4} - 1\frac{2}{3} = 3\frac{1}{12}$

(Total 3 marks)

13 Show that $3\frac{1}{3} \div 7\frac{1}{2} = \frac{4}{9}$

(Total 3 marks)

14 Show that $4\frac{1}{6} - 2\frac{4}{5} = 1\frac{11}{30}$

(Total 3 marks)

15 Show that $6\frac{2}{3} \div 1\frac{7}{8} = 3\frac{5}{9}$

(Total 3 marks)

16 Last season, Hodder Hurricanes won $\frac{5}{12}$ of its matches, drew $\frac{2}{9}$ and lost the rest.
Show that it lost $\frac{13}{36}$ of its matches.

(Total 3 marks)

17 Of the teachers in a school, $\frac{3}{4}$ are women.
Of the women teachers in the school, $\frac{5}{6}$ are married.
Work out the fraction of teachers in the school who are married women.
Give your fraction in its simplest form.

(Total 2 marks)

18 Pat's dog eats $\frac{2}{3}$ of a tin of food each day.
She has 8 tins of dog food.
How many days will the 8 tins last?

(Total 2 marks)

19 Chloe, Daisy and Emily share some money.
Chloe receives $\frac{5}{8}$ of the money.
Daisy receives $\frac{1}{6}$ of the money.
Show that Emily receives $\frac{5}{24}$ of the money.

(Total 3 marks)

20 $\frac{7}{12}$ of the passengers on a coach are boys.
The rest of the passengers are girls.
35 of the passengers are boys.
How many of the passengers are girls?

(Total 3 marks)

21 $\frac{3}{4}$ of Joshua's books are paperbacks.

$\frac{4}{9}$ of his paperback books are science fiction.

What fraction of his books are science fiction paperbacks?
Give your fraction in its simplest form.

(Total 2 marks)

22 $\frac{8}{9}$ of an iceberg lies below the water surface.

Calculate the total volume of the iceberg, if 13 200 m^3 of the iceberg lies below the water surface.

(Total 2 marks)

23 $\frac{5}{9}$ of the students in a school are girls.

$\frac{3}{5}$ of these girls own a bicycle.

$\frac{3}{4}$ of the boys in the school own a bicycle.

What fraction of the students in the school own a bicycle?
Give your fraction in its simplest form.

(Total 3 marks)

24 A bag contains only red beads, white beads and blue beads.

$\frac{5}{12}$ of the beads are red.

$\frac{3}{8}$ of the beads are white.

Work out the smallest possible number of beads that the bag could contain.

(Total 2 marks)

25 Lian bought 450 shirts to sell in her shop.
She paid $10 for each shirt.

In May, she sold $\frac{7}{9}$ of the 450 shirts.
She sold these shirts at $18 each.

In June, she reduced the price of each shirt by $\frac{1}{3}$.
She sold the remaining shirts at this price.

a) Calculate the total profit that Lian made on the shirts. **(4)**
b) Express her total profit as a fraction of the amount she paid for the shirts.
Give your fraction in its simplest form. **(1)**

(Total 5 marks)

4 Percentages

1   Express 63 as a percentage of 350

                                        (Total 2 marks)

2   Express 42 seconds as a percentage of 5 minutes.

                                        (Total 3 marks)

3   Benita's weekly pay was increased from £450 to £468
    Work out the percentage increase in Benita's weekly pay.

                                        (Total 3 marks)

4   Paulo invested $7500 at an interest rate of 5.4% per year.
    Work out the total amount in his account after one year.

                                        (Total 3 marks)

5   In a sale, normal prices are reduced by 12%.
    a)   The normal price of a case is £45
        Work out the sale price of the case.   **(3)**
    b)   The price of a computer is reduced by £69
        Work out the normal price of the computer.   **(3)**

                                        (Total 6 marks)

6   Salim invested an amount of money at 6% interest.
    After one year, interest was added to his account.
    The amount in his account was then £901
    Work out the amount of money Salim invested.

                                        (Total 3 marks)

7   Of the number of people a company employs, 64% are men.
    The company employs 112 men.
    Work out the number of people the company employs.

                                        (Total 3 marks)

8   An art dealer bought a painting for £2500 and sold it for £3300
    Work out her percentage profit.

                                        (Total 3 marks)

9 Magda got 54 out of 75 in a science test.
   a) Work out 54 out of 75 as a percentage.   **(2)**

   Dwayne got 45% of the total marks in a history test.
   Dwayne got 63 marks.
   b) Work out the total number of marks for the history test.   **(3)**

                                                 (Total 5 marks)

10 A flight normally costs £650
   It is reduced by 18%.
   How much will the flight now cost?

                                                 (Total 3 marks)

11 Jack bought a computer for $875 and later sold it for $735
   Work out his percentage loss.

                                                 (Total 3 marks)

12 In a sale, normal prices are reduced by 35%.
   The sale price of a clock is £78
   Work out the normal price of the clock.

                                                 (Total 3 marks)

13 During 2006, the population of Kenya increased from 34 708 000 to 36 914 000
   Calculate the percentage increase in Kenya's population.
   Give your answer correct to 1 decimal place.

                                                 (Total 3 marks)

14 Linton's salary is £28 000
   His salary is increased by 4.5%.
   Work out Linton's new salary.

                                                 (Total 3 marks)

15 Before dieting, Kate's weight was 75 kg.
   After dieting, her weight was 66 kg.
   Work out Kate's percentage weight loss.

                                                 (Total 3 marks)

16 David and Gwen bought a house.
   After one year, its value had increased by 9% to £196 200
   Work out the value of the house when they bought it.

                                                 (Total 3 marks)

17 70.9% of the Earth's surface is covered by water.
The area of the Earth's surface covered by water is $362\,000\,000\ km^2$.
Calculate the total surface area of the Earth.
Give your answer correct to 2 significant figures.

(Total 3 marks)

18 100 g of Bran Flakes contains 10.8 g of protein.
The Recommended Daily Amount (RDA) of protein is 90 g.
  a) What percentage of the RDA of protein is provided by 100 g of Bran Flakes? **(2)**

100 g of Bran Flakes contains 16.1 mg of iron.
The Recommended Daily Amount (RDA) of iron is 14 mg.
  b) What percentage of the RDA of iron is provided by 100 g of Bran Flakes? **(2)**

100 g of Bran Flakes contains 13.6 g of fibre.
13.6 g is 56.7% of the RDA of fibre.
  c) Calculate the RDA of fibre.
    Give your answer correct to 2 significant figures. **(3)**

(Total 7 marks)

19 The number of candidates who took maths IGCSE was 88.9% greater in May 2007 than the number of candidates in May 2006
In May 2007, 18 800 candidates took maths IGCSE.
Calculate the number of candidates who took maths IGCSE in May 2006

(Total 3 marks)

20 *Solarhols* make a cancellation charge if a customer cancels a holiday less than six weeks before departure.
The cancellation charge is a percentage of the cost of the holiday.
Hassan booked a holiday with *Solarhols*.
He cancelled his holiday three weeks before the departure date.
He had to pay a cancellation charge of 40% of the cost of the holiday.
His cancellation charge was £408
Work out the cost of his holiday.

(Total 3 marks)

21 Tamsin bought a car.
The cost of the car was $8640
She paid a deposit of 35% of the cost of the car.
She paid the remainder of the cost in 36 equal monthly instalments.
Work out the monthly instalment Tamsin paid.

(Total 4 marks)

22 Rohan opened an account with £800 at the London Bank.
    After one year, the bank paid him interest.
    He then had £836 in his account.
    Work out, as a percentage, London Bank's interest rate.

                                                                          (Total 3 marks)

23 The length of a new curtain was 85 cm.
    When it was washed, the curtain shrank by 4%.
    Work out the length of the curtain after it had been washed.

                                                                          (Total 3 marks)

24 Usave Motor Insurance reduces the premiums its customers pay for car insurance by a
    certain percentage, according to the number of consecutive years for which the
    customer has not made a claim.
    This percentage reduction in premiums is called the 'No-claims bonus'.
    The table shows Usave's No-claims bonuses.

Number of consecutive years without a claim	No-claims bonus
1	35%
2	45%
3	55%
4	60%
5 or more	65%

Leela has not made a claim during the last 2 years.
Without the No-claims bonus, her premium would be £360
a) Calculate her premium with the No-claims bonus.   **(3)**

Dean has not made a claim during the last 7 years.
With the No-claims bonus, his premium is £182
b) Calculate his premium without the No-claims bonus.   **(3)**

                                                                          (Total 6 marks)

25 Sachin invested £6000 for 2 years at 5% per annum compound interest.
    Calculate the value of his investment at the end of 2 years.

                                                                          (Total 3 marks)

26 $5000 is invested for 3 years at 4% per annum compound interest.
    Work out the total interest earned over the 3 years.

                                                                          (Total 3 marks)

27 Liz bought a car for £12 500
      The car depreciated by 10% each year.
      Work out the value of the car 4 years after she bought it.

                                                                    (Total 3 marks)

28 Rajiv invested $20 000 at 7% per annum compound interest.
      After n years, the value of his investment had grown to $30 014.61
      Find the value of n.

                                                                    (Total 3 marks)

29 Emma invested an amount of money.
      Compound interest was paid at a rate of 4.6% per annum.
      After 2 years, the value of her investment was £30 088.19
      Calculate the amount she invested.

                                                                    (Total 3 marks)

30 Ben invested an amount of money at 5.2% per annum compound interest.
      Calculate the number of years after which the value of his investment had doubled.

                                                                    (Total 3 marks)

31 An increase of 30% is followed by an increase of 40%.
      Find the total percentage increase.

                                                                    (Total 3 marks)

32 The value of a new car decreases by 20% in the first year and by 15% in the second
      year.
      Calculate the total percentage decrease in its value in the two years.

                                                                    (Total 3 marks)

33 Leela says that a decrease of 35% followed by an increase of 60% is the same as an
      increase of 25%.
      Is Leela correct? You must show working to justify your answer.

                                                                    (Total 3 marks)

34 When *Easy PC* sells computers at their normal prices, it makes a profit of 30%.
      In a sale, normal prices are reduced by 10%.
      Calculate the percentage profit on a computer sold in the sale.

                                                                    (Total 3 marks)

35 Find the total percentage change when an increase of 60% is followed by a
      decrease of 50% and then by a decrease of 10%.

                                                                    (Total 4 marks)

5 Ratio and proportion

1 The recommended daily amount of fibre for men is 24 grams.
The recommended daily amount of carbohydrates for men is 300 grams.
Find the ratio of the recommended daily amount of carbohydrates for men to the
recommended daily amount of fibre for men.
Give your ratio in the form $1 : n$

(Total 2 marks)

2 The population of Malta is 4×10^5
The population of the United Kingdom is 6×10^7
Find the ratio of the population of Malta to the population of the United Kingdom.
Give your ratio in the form $1 : n$

(Total 2 marks)

3 The length of an aeroplane is 7.5 m.
A scale model is made of the aeroplane.
The length of the scale model is 30 cm.
a) Express the scale of the model in the form $1 : n$ **(3)**

The wingspan of the scale model is 36 cm.
b) Work out the wingspan of the real aeroplane.
Give your answer in metres. **(3)**

(Total 6 marks)

4 A total of 64 320 people watched the football match between United and City.
The ratio of United supporters to City supporters was $15 : 1$
Work out the number of United supporters who watched the match.

(Total 2 marks)

5 John and Pavinder share some money in the ratio $5 : 7$
John receives $240
Work out the amount of money that Pavinder receives.

(Total 2 marks)

6 Brass is made from copper and zinc in the ratio $13 : 7$ by weight.
a) Work out the weight of copper and the weight of zinc in 5 kg of brass. **(3)**

A brass ornament contains 350 grams of zinc.
b) Work out the weight of copper in the ornament. **(2)**

(Total 5 marks)

7   The lengths of the sides of an isosceles triangle are in the ratios $3:3:5$
The length of the equal sides of the triangle is 6.6 cm.
Work out the perimeter of the triangle.

(Total 3 marks)

8   The sizes of the angles of a triangle are in the ratios $2:3:7$
Work out the size of the obtuse angle of the triangle.

(Total 3 marks)

9   Rajesh runs a distance of $2\frac{2}{3}$ km each day.
How far, in kilometres, does Rajesh run in 7 days?
Give your answer as a mixed number.

(Total 2 marks)

10 The amount of money Zhanna is paid is directly proportional to the number of
computers she sells. Last month Zhanna sold 28 computers and was paid $1512
  a) Work out the number of computers Zhanna sold when she was paid $2106   **(2)**
  b) Work out the amount of money Zhanna is paid for selling 21 computers.   **(2)**

(Total 4 marks)

11 The scale of a map is $1:5\,000\,000$
On the map, the distance between two airports is 3.6 cm.
  a) Work out the real distance between the airports.
     Give your answer in kilometres.   **(3)**

The real distance between two railway stations is 30 km.
  b) Work out the distance on the map between the two railway stations.   **(2)**

(Total 5 marks)

12 Here are the ingredients needed to make a pie for 4 people.

<u>Ingredients for 4 people</u>
150 g of pastry
450 g of potatoes
220 g of onions
320 g of bacon

Work out the amount of each ingredient needed to make a pie for 10 people.

(Total 3 marks)

13 Kurt went on holiday to England.
He changed €1800 to pounds.
The exchange rate was €1 = £0.69
a) Work out the number of pounds Kurt received.   **(2)**

Kurt returned home with £198
He changed his £198 to euros.
The new exchange rate was €1 = £0.66
b) Work out the number of euros Kurt received.   **(2)**

(Total 4 marks)

6 Standard form

1 **a)** Write the number 230 000 in standard form. **(1)**
   b) Write 6.3×10^{-3} as an ordinary number. **(1)**

   (Total 2 marks)

2 **a)** Write the number 0.000 47 in standard form. **(1)**
   b) Write 3.7×10^6 as an ordinary number. **(1)**
   c) Work out the value of $\dfrac{5 \times 10^3}{8 \times 10^{-5}}$

   Give your answer in standard form. **(1)**

   (Total 3 marks)

3 The distance between Mercury and the Sun is 58 000 000 km.
   a) Write the number 58 000 000 in standard form. **(1)**

   Uranus is 50 times as far from the Sun as Mercury
   b) Calculate the distance between Uranus and the Sun.
   Give your answer in standard form. **(2)**

   (Total 3 marks)

4 Work out the value of $(6 \times 10^5) \times (8 \times 10^{-4})$.
   Give your answer in standard form.

   (Total 2 marks)

5 Work out the value of $(7.2 \times 10^4) + (4.7 \times 10^3)$.
   Give your answer in standard form.

   (Total 2 marks)

6 The age of the Universe is approximately 15 000 million years.
   a) Write the number 15 000 million in standard form. **(1)**

   1 gigayear $= 10^9$ years.
   b) Express the age of the Universe in gigayears. **(2)**

   (Total 3 marks)

7 The mass of a proton is 0.000 000 000 000 000 000 000 001 67 grams.
  a) Write the number 0.000 000 000 000 000 000 000 001 67 in standard form. **(1)**

The mass of a proton is 1850 times greater than the mass of an electron.
  b) Calculate the mass, in grams, of an electron.
  Give your answer in standard form correct to 2 significant figures. **(2)**

(Total 3 marks)

8 $P = 2a + 5b$
$a = 3.5 \times 10^6$ and $b = 2.7 \times 10^7$
Work out the value of P.
Give your answer in standard form.

(Total 2 marks)

9 A spherical planet has a radius of 6800 km.
Calculate the surface area, in km^2, of the planet.
Give your answer in standard form correct to 2 significant figures.

(Total 3 marks)

10 $y = \dfrac{a + b}{ab}$

$a = 2 \times 10^4$ and $b = 8 \times 10^5$

Work out the value of y.
Give your answer in standard form correct to 3 significant figures.

(Total 3 marks)

11 A supercomputer can perform 12 300 000 000 000 calculations per second.
  a) Write the number 12 300 000 000 000 in standard form. **(1)**
  b) Work out the number of calculations this computer can perform in 4 hours.
  Give your answer in standard form correct to 2 significant figures. **(2)**

1 nanosecond $= 10^{-9}$ seconds.
  c) Work out the time, in nanoseconds, this computer takes to perform one calculation.
  Give your answer in standard form correct to 2 significant figures. **(2)**

(Total 5 marks)

12 $F = 3p - 4q$
$p = 2 \times 10^{-5}$ and $q = 8 \times 10^{-6}$
Work out the value of F.
Give your answer in standard form.

(Total 2 marks)

13 The Andromeda Galaxy is the most distant galaxy that can be seen with the naked eye from Earth.

The distance from the Andromeda Galaxy to Earth is 2.19×10^{19} km.

Light travels 9.46×10^{12} km in a year.

Calculate the time, in years, light takes to travel from the Andromeda Galaxy to Earth.

Give your answer in standard form correct to 2 significant figures.

(Total 3 marks)

14 $T = \dfrac{xy}{x - y}$

$x = 5.3 \times 10^{-3}$ and $y = 6.7 \times 10^{-4}$

Work out the value of T.

Give your answer in standard form correct to 3 significant figures.

(Total 3 marks)

15 1 litre of paint covers an area of 12 m^2.

Work out the thickness, in centimetres, of the coat of paint.

Give your answer in standard form correct to 2 significant figures.

(Total 4 marks)

16 $p^2 = \dfrac{2a}{b}$

$a = 7.3 \times 10^{13}$ and $b = 2.9 \times 10^{-4}$

Work out the value of p.

Give your answer in standard form correct to 2 significant figures.

(Total 3 marks)

17 The mass of an atom can be expressed in atomic mass units.

1 atomic mass unit (amu) $= 1.66 \times 10^{-27}$ kg.

a) The weight of 1 atom of carbon 12 is 12 amu.

Express 12 amu in kg.

Give your answer in standard form.   **(2)**

b) The weight of 1 atom of gold is 3.27×10^{-25} kg.

Express 3.27×10^{-25} kg in amu.

Give your answer correct to the nearest whole number.   **(2)**

(Total 4 marks)

18 1 light year $= 9.46 \times 10^{12}$ km.
    a) The distance from the Earth to the star Alpha Centauri is 4.35 light years.
        Work out the distance, in kilometres, from the Earth to the star Alpha Centauri.
        Give your answer in standard form correct to 2 significant figures.   **(2)**
    b) The distance from the Earth to the centre of the Milky Way is 2.65×10^{17} km.
        Express 2.65×10^{17} km in light years.
        Give your answer in standard form correct to 2 significant figures.   **(2)**

                                                             (Total 4 marks)

19 Muons and taus are subatomic particles.
    The lifetime of a muon is 2.2×10^{-6} seconds.
    a) Write 2.2×10^{-6} as an ordinary number.   **(1)**

    The lifetime of a muon is 7.56×10^{6} times greater than the lifetime of a tau.
    b) Calculate the lifetime, in seconds, of a tau.
        Give your answer in standard form correct to 3 significant figures.   **(2)**

                                                             (Total 3 marks)

20 The mass of the Earth is 5.97×10^{21} tonnes.
    The mass of the Moon is 7.36×10^{19} tonnes.
    a) How many times greater is the mass of the Earth than the mass of the Moon?
        Give your answer correct to the nearest whole number.   **(2)**

    The mass of Mars is 11% of the mass of the Earth.
    b) Work out the difference in mass, in tonnes, between Mars and the Moon.
        Give your answer in standard form correct to 2 significant figures.   **(2)**

                                                             (Total 4 marks)

21 $x = 2 \times 10^{m}$ and $y = 3 \times 10^{n}$ where m and n are integers.
    Find an expression, in standard form, for xy.

                                                               (Total 2 marks)

22 $x = 6 \times 10^{m}$ and $y = 4 \times 10^{n}$ where m and n are integers.
    Find an expression, in standard form, for:

    a) xy **b)** $\dfrac{x}{y}$

                                                            (Total 4 marks)

23 $x = 7 \times 10^{n}$ where n is an integer.
    Find an expression, in standard form, for x^2
    Give your expression as simply as possible.

                                                               (Total 3 marks)

24 $x = 5 \times 10^m$ and $y = 8 \times 10^n$ where m and n are integers.

Find an expression, in standard form, for $\dfrac{x}{y}$.

(Total 3 marks)

25 $3.2 \times 10^8 + a \times 10^7 = 3.8 \times 10^8$
Find the value of a.

(Total 2 marks)

26 $(7 \times 10^5) \times (a \times 10^n) = 6.3 \times 10^{-4}$ where $1 \leqslant a < 10$ and n is an integer.
Find the value of a and the value of n.

(Total 3 marks)

27 $\dfrac{7 \times 10^6}{a \times 10^n} = 8.75 \times 10^9$ where $1 \leqslant a < 10$ and n is an integer.

Find the value of a and the value of n.

(Total 3 marks)

28 $x = 4 \times 10^m$ and $y = 2 \times 10^n$ where m and n are integers.

$xy = 8 \times 10^2$ and $\dfrac{x}{y} = 2 \times 10^8$

Find
a) the value of m **b)** the value of n.

(Total 4 marks)

7 Degree of accuracy

1 Sophie wants to work out an estimate for the value of $2.8 + 34.1 \times 0.37$ without using a calculator.

Write down, for each number, an approximate value she could use.

(Total 2 marks)

2 Dilip wants to work out an estimate for the value of $\dfrac{42.7 \times 9.3}{27.2}$ without using a calculator.

   a) Round each number in Dilip's calculation to 1 significant figure. **(2)**

   b) Use your rounded numbers to work out an estimate for the value

      of $\dfrac{42.7 \times 9.3}{27.2}$ **(1)**

   c) Without using a calculator, explain why your answer to part **b)** should be smaller than the exact answer. **(1)**

(Total 4 marks)

3 Alice wants to work out an estimate for the value of $\dfrac{36.8 \times 78.2}{0.53 \times 4.2}$ without using a calculator.

   a) Round each number in Alice's calculation to 1 significant figure. **(2)**

   b) Use your rounded numbers to work out an estimate for the value

      of $\dfrac{36.8 \times 78.2}{0.53 \times 4.2}$

      Give your answer correct to 1 significant figure. **(2)**

   c) Without using a calculator, explain why your answer to part **b)** should be larger than the exact answer. **(2)**

(Total 6 marks)

4 The weight of a cat is 6.4 kg, correct to 2 significant figures.

   a) Write down the upper bound for the weight of the cat.

   b) Write down the lower bound for the weight of the cat.

(Total 2 marks)

5 The diameter of a CD is 11.8 cm, correct to 3 significant figures.

   a) Write down the upper bound for the diameter of a CD.

   b) Write down the lower bound for the diameter of a CD.

(Total 2 marks)

6 The weight of a book is 0.57 kg, correct to 2 decimal places.
Calculate the lower bound for the weight of 40 of these books.

(Total 2 marks)

7 The length of a side of a square is 7.4 cm, correct to 1 decimal place.
a) Work out
    i) the upper bound for the perimeter of the square
    ii) the lower bound for the perimeter of the square. **(3)**
b) **i)** Give the perimeter of the square to an appropriate degree of accuracy.
    ii) Explain how you obtained your answer. **(2)**

(Total 5 marks)

8 The distance from London to Birmingham is 179 km, correct to the nearest kilometre.
On Monday, Sean drove from London to Birmingham and back.
He repeated the journey on Tuesday and on Wednesday.
Calculate the upper bound for the total distance Sean drove.

(Total 2 marks)

9 Correct to 1 significant figure, $x = 9$ and $y = 6$
a) Calculate the lower bound for the value of $x - y$. **(2)**
b) Calculate the upper bound for the value of xy. **(2)**

(Total 4 marks)

10 The perimeter of a regular pentagon is 24 cm, correct to 2 significant figures.
Calculate the lower bound for the length of each side.

(Total 2 marks)

11 Correct to the nearest centimetre, Alan's height is 1.76 m and Nina's height is 1.64 m.
Calculate the upper bound for the difference between their heights.

(Total 3 marks)

12 Correct to 1 significant figure, $x = 8$ and $y = 2$

Calculate the lower bound for the value of $\dfrac{x}{y}$.

(Total 3 marks)

13 The circumference of a circle is 23.4 cm, correct to 3 significant figures.
a) Calculate the upper bound for the diameter of the circle.
    Write down all the figures on your calculator display. **(2)**
b) Give the diameter of the circle to an appropriate degree of accuracy.
    You must show working to explain how you obtained your answer. **(2)**

(Total 4 marks)

14 Correct to 2 significant figures, the area of a rectangle is 29 cm².
Correct to 2 significant figures, the width of the rectangle is 4.8 cm.
Calculate the upper bound for the length of the rectangle.
Write down all the figures on your calculator display.

(Total 3 marks)

15 When full, a car's petrol tank holds 54 litres, correct to the nearest litre.
Correct to 1 decimal place, the car travels 15.8 km on one litre of petrol.
Calculate the lower bound for the distance the car will travel on a full tank of petrol.

(Total 3 marks)

16 Sinead ran 68 metres, correct to the nearest metre.
Her time for the run was 9.8 seconds, correct to the nearest tenth of a second.
Calculate the upper bound for her average speed in m/s.

(Total 3 marks)

17 A crane can lift a load of 3210 kg, correct to 3 significant figures.
The weight of a box is 92 kg, correct to the nearest kilogram.
Calculate the greatest number of these boxes the crane can lift.

(Total 3 marks)

18

Diagram **NOT**
accurately drawn

In triangle ABC, angle $ABC = 90°$.
$BC = 11$ cm, correct to the nearest centimetre.
$AC = 17$ cm, correct to the nearest centimetre.
Calculate the upper bound for the length of AB.

(Total 4 marks)

19 The formula $I = \dfrac{W}{h^2}$ gives the Body Mass Index, I, of a person with weight

W kilograms and height h metres.
Jose's weight is 73 kg, correct to the nearest kilogram.
His height is 1.79 m, correct to the nearest centimetre.
Calculate Jose's Body Mass Index to an appropriate degree of accuracy.
You must show working to explain how you obtained your answer.

(Total 5 marks)

20

Diagram **NOT** accurately drawn

Triangle ABC is right-angled at B.
$AB = 7.3$ cm, correct to 2 significant figures.
$BC = 5.7$ cm, correct to 2 significant figures.
The line AB is horizontal.
Calculate the gradient of the line AC to an appropriate degree of accuracy.
You must show working to explain how you obtained your answer.

(Total 5 marks)

8 Set language and notation

1 $A = \{1, 2, 3, 4, 6\}$
  $B = \{1, 3, 5, 8\}$
  a) List the members of the set:
    i) $A \cup B$ **ii)** $A \cap B$.   **(2)**
  b) Explain clearly the meaning of $5 \notin A$.   **(1)**

           (Total 3 marks)

---

2 **a)** $A = \{$Quadrilaterals whose diagonals cross at right angles$\}$
    $B = \{$Cyclic quadrilaterals$\}$
    Write down the mathematical name for the quadrilaterals in:
    i) A **ii)** $A \cap B$.   **(2)**
  b) $\mathscr{E} = \{$Positive whole numbers less than 20$\}$
    $P = \{$Multiples of 2$\}$
    $Q = \{$Multiples of 7$\}$
    i) Explain why it is not true that $21 \in Q$.
    ii) Is it true that $P \cap Q = \varnothing$? Explain your answer.   **(3)**

           (Total 5 marks)

---

3 $\mathscr{E} = \{1, 2, 3, 4, 5, 6, 7, 8, 9, 10\}$
  $P = \{1, 2, 5, 7, 9, 10\}$
  a) List the members of P'.   **(1)**
  The set Q satisfies both $Q \subset P$ **and** $n(Q) = 4$
  b) List the members of **one** set Q which satisfies both these conditions.   **(2)**

           (Total 3 marks)

---

4 $\mathscr{E} = \{$positive integers less than 16$\}$
  $A = \{x : x \geqslant 9\}$
  $B = \{x : x < 14\}$
  a) List the members of the set:
    i) $A \cap B$ **ii)** B'.   **(2)**
  b) What is $(A \cup B)'$?   **(1)**

           (Total 3 marks)

---

5 $P = \{$Prime numbers between 20 and 30$\}$
  $M = \{$Multiples of 7 between 20 and 30$\}$
  a) List the members of $P \cup M$.   **(2)**
  b) What is $M \cap P$?   **(1)**
  c) Is it true that $27 \in P$? Explain your answer.   **(1)**

           (Total 4 marks)

6 $\mathscr{E} = \{$odd numbers less than 30$\}$
$P = \{$factors of 36$\}$
$Q = \{$factors of 60$\}$
a) **i)** Explain why $12 \notin P \cap Q$.
   ii) List the members of Q.   **(2)**
b) List the members of $P \cap Q$.   **(2)**

(Total 4 marks)

7

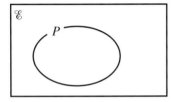

Set P is shown on the Venn diagram.
Two sets, Q and R, are such that:

$P \subset R$
$P \cap R \cap Q = \varnothing$
$R \cap Q = Q$

Complete a copy of the Venn diagram to show set Q and set R.

(Total 3 marks)

8

Statements
$A = B$ $B \subset A$ $A' \cup B = \mathscr{E}$ $A \cap B' = A$ $A \cap B = B$

Choose a statement from the box that describes the relationship between sets A and B.

a)

b)

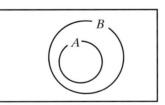

(Total 2 marks)

9 $\mathscr{E}$ = {positive whole numbers less than 100}
A = {multiples of 5}
B = {multiples of 2}

Sets A and B are represented by the circles in the Venn diagram:

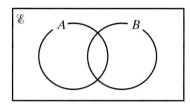

a) i) Copy the diagram and shade the region that represents the set $(A \cup B)'$.
ii) Write down two members of the set $(A \cup B)'$.
iii) Write down two members of the set $A \cap B'$. **(3)**

C = {multiples of 6}
b) i) Copy the diagram and draw a circle, C, to represent the set C.
ii) Find $n(A \cap B \cap C)$. **(2)**

(Total 5 marks)

10

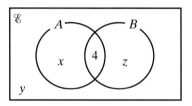

In the Venn diagram, 4, x, y and z represent the **numbers** of elements.
$n(\mathscr{E}) = 30$ $n(A) = 9$ $n(B') = 20$
a) Find the value of:
 i) x **ii)** y **iii)** z **(3)**
b) Find
 i) $n(A' \cup B)$ **ii)** $n((A \cup B)')$ **iii)** $n(A \cap B \cap B')$ **(3)**

(Total 6 marks)

11 Each student in a Year 11 group studies at least one of French, German and Spanish.

15 students study German only.
25 students study Spanish only.
20 students study French only.
6 students study German and Spanish but not French.
13 students study French and Spanish.
10 students study French and German.
x students study all three languages.

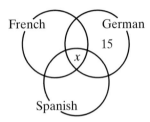

a) Write down an expression, in terms of *x*, for:
   i) the number of students who study French and Spanish but not German
   ii) the number of students who study French and German but not Spanish. **(2)**

There are 81 students in the group.
b) Find the value of *x*. **(3)**

(Total 5 marks)

12 There are 32 students in a class.

18 students have a brother.
10 students have both a brother and a sister.
9 students have neither a brother nor a sister.

Find the number of students in the class who have a sister.

(Total 4 marks)

Algebra

9 Algebraic manipulation

1 **a)** Simplify $a + 4b - 6a + 2b - 1$ **(2)**
   b) Multiply out $3(2p + 7)$ **(1)**
   c) Factorise $9x + 12$ **(1)**

(Total 4 marks)

2 **a)** Expand $x(3x + 2)$ **(2)**
   b) Expand and simplify $4(3x - 1) + 3(x + 5)$ **(2)**
   c) Expand and simplify $(y + 4)(y + 2)$ **(2)**

(Total 6 marks)

3 **a)** Multiply out and simplify $3(2x + 1) + 2(x + 4)$ **(2)**
   b) Multiply out $x(5x + 4y)$ **(2)**
   c) Factorise $12y - 8$ **(1)**

(Total 5 marks)

4 **a)** Expand and simplify $2(2y + 1) + 5(y - 3)$ **(2)**
   b) Factorise $15 - 20p$ **(1)**
   c) Expand and simplify $(x - 6)(x + 1)$ **(2)**

(Total 5 marks)

5 **a)** Expand $q(7q^2 + 5)$ **(2)**
   b) Expand and simplify $5(y + 1) - 4(2y + 3)$ **(2)**
   c) Factorise $x^2 - 6x$ **(2)**

(Total 6 marks)

6 **a)** Expand and simplify $7(y - 1) - 6(2y - 3)$ **(2)**
   b) Expand $2x(x - 3y)$ **(2)**

(Total 4 marks)

7 **a)** Expand and simplify $3(4x - 5) + 2(x - 3)$ **(2)**
   b) Expand $3p^3(p - 1)$ **(2)**
   c) Expand and simplify $(y - 1)(y - 5)$ **(2)**

(Total 6 marks)

8   **a)**   Factorise completely $18x - 8x^2$ **(2)**
   b)   Factorise $x^2 + 9x + 20$ **(2)**

(**Total 4 marks**)

9   **a)**   Expand and simplify $(3p - 2q)(2p + 5q)$ **(2)**
   b)   Factorise $x^2 - 16$ **(2)**

(**Total 4 marks**)

10   Factorise $x^2 - 8x - 20$

(**Total 2 marks**)

11   Factorise $2x^2 + 9x - 5$

(**Total 2 marks**)

12   Factorise completely $8x^2 + 10x - 12$

(**Total 3 marks**)

13   Factorise completely $12x^2 - 75$

(**Total 2 marks**)

14   Simplify $\dfrac{2(x + 2)^2}{8(x + 2)}$

(**Total 2 marks**)

15   Simplify fully $\dfrac{x^2 + 2x - 3}{x^2 - 1}$

(**Total 3 marks**)

16   Simplify fully $\dfrac{x^2 - 9}{x^2 - 9x - 36}$

(**Total 3 marks**)

17   Simplify fully $\dfrac{x^2 + 5x + 6}{x^2 + x - 6}$

(**Total 3 marks**)

18   Express the algebraic fraction $\dfrac{2x^2 + 11x + 12}{4x^2 - 9}$ as simply as possible.

(**Total 3 marks**)

19 Simplify fully $\dfrac{2}{x-2} + \dfrac{3x-4}{x^2-5x+6}$

(Total 6 marks)

20 Simplify fully $\dfrac{3}{x-3} - \dfrac{x+18}{x^2+x-12}$

(Total 6 marks)

21 a) Factorise $9x^2 - 1$ **(1)**

    b) Hence express as a product of its prime factors:

      i) 899

      ii) 8.99×10^4 **(4)**

(Total 5 marks)

10 Expressions and formulae

1   Work out the value of $x^2 - 6x$ when $x = -3$

(Total 2 marks)

2   Work out the value of $6p - 2pq$ when $p = -3$ and $q = 4$

(Total 2 marks)

3 $u = \dfrac{fv}{v - f}$

Work out the value of u when $f = 14.08$ and $v = -6.4$

(Total 3 marks)

4   The formula for the area, A, of an ellipse is

$$A = \pi ab$$

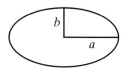

Calculate the value of a when $A = 24.6$ and $b = 1.7$
Give your answer correct to 1 decimal place.

(Total 2 marks)

5 $a = \dfrac{b}{c}$

Work out the value of a when $b = \dfrac{4}{9}$ and $c = \dfrac{5}{6}$

(Total 2 marks)

6   Simon repairs computers. The word formula gives the fee, in pounds, that Simon charges to repair a computer.

Fee = 40 × number of hours repair takes + 32

Simon charges a fee of F pounds for a repair that takes H hours.
Write down a formula for F in terms of H.

(Total 2 marks)

7 Here is a pattern of shapes made from regular hexagons of side 1 cm:

| Shape | Shape | Shape | Shape |
| number 1 | number 2 | number 3 | number 4 |

This rule can be used to find the perimeter, in cm, of a shape in this pattern.

> Double the Shape number
> then add 1
> and then multiply your answer by 2

P cm is the perimeter of Shape number n.

a) Find the perimeter when the Shape number is 12   **(2)**

b) Write down a formula for P in terms of n.   **(3)**

c) Make n the subject of the formula in part **b)**.   **(3)**

(Total 8 marks)

---

8 Make r the subject of the formula $A = \pi r^2$

(Total 2 marks)

---

9 Make h the subject of the formula $y = m(x - h)$

(Total 3 marks)

---

10 Make s the subject of the formula $t = \sqrt{\dfrac{2s}{a}}$

(Total 3 marks)

---

11 Make x the subject of $3(x + 2b) = y(2 - 5x)$

(Total 4 marks)

---

12 Make x the subject of the formula $y = \dfrac{a}{x + a}$

(Total 4 marks)

---

13 Make r the subject of the formula $T = a(R + r)(R - r) + t$

(Total 4 marks)

14 A square with side of length L has area A and perimeter P
A and P are given by the formulae

$$A = L^2$$
$$P = 4L$$

a) Work out the value of P when $A = 121$ **(2)**
b) Find a formula for P in terms of A. **(2)**
c) Find a formula for A in terms of P. **(2)**

(Total 6 marks)

11 Linear equations and simultaneous equations

1 Solve $4x - 1 = x + 7$

(Total 2 marks)

2 Solve $8x + 3 = 2x - 2$

(Total 3 marks)

3 Solve the equation $2y + 7 = 6y + 5$

(Total 3 marks)

4 Solve $5(x - 3) = 45$

(Total 3 marks)

5 Solve $4(2x + 5) = 32$

(Total 3 marks)

6 Solve $2(x + 4) = 9$

(Total 3 marks)

7 Solve $5 - 8x = 8$

(Total 3 marks)

8 Solve $9 - 4x = 7$

(Total 3 marks)

9 Solve $\dfrac{5x + 3}{6} = 2$

(Total 3 marks)

10 Solve $\dfrac{9 + 2x}{4} = 3x + 2$

(Total 4 marks)

11 Solve $\dfrac{y + 3}{4} + \dfrac{2y - 3}{2} = 2$

(Total 4 marks)

12 Solve $4(3p + 1) = 15p + 8$

(Total 3 marks)

13 The diagram shows the lengths, in centimetres, of the sides of a triangle.

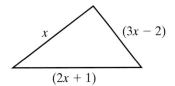

Diagram **NOT**
accurately drawn

The perimeter of the triangle is 14 cm.
a) Use this information to write an equation in x.
b) Solve your equation.
c) Find the length of the longest side of the triangle.

(Total 4 marks)

14 Berto's age is x years. Rico's age is four times Berto's age.
In 10 years' time Rico's age will be twice Berto's age.
a) Use this information to write an equation in x. **(3)**
b) Solve your equation to find Berto's present age. **(3)**

(Total 6 marks)

15

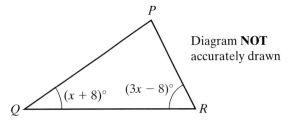

Diagram **NOT**
accurately drawn

PQR is a triangle.
Angle $Q = (x + 8)°$ and angle $R = (3x - 8)°$
The size of angle R is twice the size of angle Q.
i) Use this information to write an equation in x.
ii) Find the size of angle P.

(Total 6 marks)

16 $y = 2x - 5$

Work out the value of x when $y = -6$

(Total 2 marks)

17 $v = u + gt$

Find the value of t when $v = 16, u = 2$ and $g = 10$

(Total 2 marks)

18 $s = ut + \frac{1}{2}at^2$

Work out the value of a when $s = 60, u = 8$ and $t = 5$

(Total 2 marks)

19 Solve the simultaneous equations:

$y = x - 4$
$y = 9x$

(Total 3 marks)

20 Solve the simultaneous equations:

$4x + 3y = 3$
$2x - 6y = 9$

(Total 3 marks)

21 Solve the simultaneous equations:

$7x - 10y = 6$
$3x - 4y = 3$

(Total 4 marks)

22 a) Solve the simultaneous equations:

$2x - 3y = 3$
$4x + 4y = 1$ **(3)**

b) Write down the coordinates of the point of intersection of the two lines whose equations are:

$2x - 3y = 3$ and
$4x + 4y = 1$ **(1)**

(Total 4 marks)

23 Work out the coordinates of the point of intersection of the line with equation $6x - 5y = 5$ and the line with equation $4x - 4y = 3$

(Total 4 marks)

12 Coordinates and graphs

1 Two points, A and B, are plotted on a grid.
  A has coordinates $(0, 4)$ and B has coordinates $(6, 10)$.
  Work out the coordinates of the midpoint of the line joining A and B.

  (Total 2 marks)

2 P has coordinates $(-1, 2)$ and X has coordinates $(0, 5)$.
  X is the midpoint of the line PQ.
  Find the coordinates of point Q.

  (Total 2 marks)

3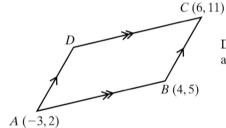

  Diagram **NOT**
  accurately drawn

  $ABCD$ is a parallelogram.
  A has coordinates $(-3, 2)$, B has coordinates $(4, 5)$ and C has coordinates $(6, 11)$.
  a) Find the coordinates of point D. **(2)**
  b) Find the coordinates of the point of intersection of the two diagonals AC and
  BD. **(2)**

  (Total 4 marks)

4 Bishen sets off from home at 12 noon to meet his grandmother at the airport.
  On the way, he remembers that he had left his mobile phone at home.
  He returns home to collect it and sets off to the airport again to meet his grandmother.
  At the airport he has to wait for her. He drives her the 10 km to her house and he then
  returns home.
  The diagram shows Bishen's distance/time graph for the 80 minute journey.

a) At what time did Bishen arrive at the airport? **(1)**
b) How many minutes did he wait at the airport? **(1)**
c) How many kilometres did Bishen travel between noon and 1320? **(1)**
d) Between which two times was Bishen driving most quickly? **(1)**
e) At what times was Bishen 10 km from the airport? **(2)**
f) Calculate Bishen's speed during his journey home from his grandmother's house.
   Give your answer in kilometres per hour. **(2)**

(Total 8 marks)

5 Xanthe cycled from her home to visit her uncle.
Xanthe stopped at a shop on the way to buy him a present.
The diagram shows her distance/time graph for the journey to her uncle's house.

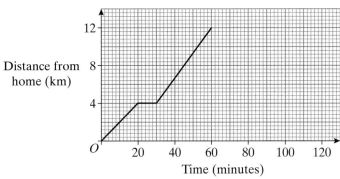

a) For how many minutes did Xanthe stop to buy the present? **(1)**
b) Find the distance from Xanthe's home to her uncle's house. **(1)**
c) Calculate the speed at which Xanthe cycled from home to the shop.
   Give your answer in kilometres per hour. **(2)**
Xanthe stayed at her uncle's house for 30 minutes.
She then travelled back home at 48 km/h in her uncle's car.
d) i) Complete a copy of the distance/time graph.
   ii) For how many minutes had Xanthe been away from home? **(4)**

(Total 8 marks)

6   The diagram shows the velocity/time graph for the first 40 seconds of a car journey.

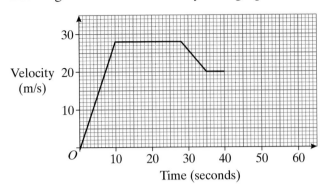

a) Find the constant acceleration of the car during the first 10 seconds.   **(2)**
b) **i)** Write down the greatest velocity of the car in the first 40 seconds.
    ii) Calculate the distance travelled by the car while it is travelling at this greatest velocity.   **(3)**

After 40 seconds the car decelerates at a constant rate of 2 m/s² and comes to rest.
c) Complete a copy of the velocity/time graph.   **(2)**

(Total 7 marks)

7   A ball is projected vertically upwards from the edge of a flat roof.
t seconds after being projected, the height of the ball above the ground is h metres.
The diagram shows the graph of h against t, for $0 \leqslant t \leqslant 5$

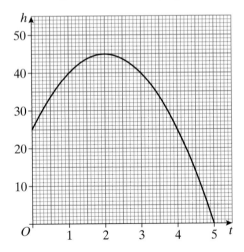

Using the graph, find:
a) the height above the ground from which the ball was projected
b) the maximum height of the ball
c) the total time for which the ball was at least 40 m above the ground.

(Total 3 marks)

13 Linear graphs

1

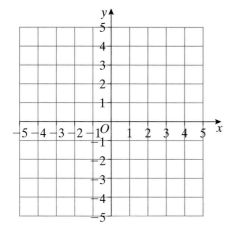

   a) On a copy of the grid, draw the line $x + y = 3$ **(1)**
   b) Find the coordinates of the point of intersection of the lines whose equations are
       $x + y = 3$ and $x = -1$ **(2)**

                                                    (Total 3 marks)

2   **a)** On a copy of the grid, draw the line $y = \frac{1}{2}x - 2$ **(3)**

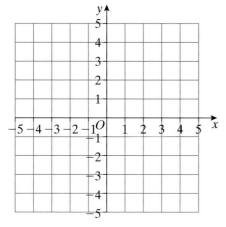

   b) Find the coordinates of the point of intersection of the lines $y = \frac{1}{2}x - 2$
       and $y = -3$ **(2)**

                                                    (Total 5 marks)

3 On a copy of the grid, draw the graph of $y = 4x + 6$ from $x = -4$ to $x = 2$

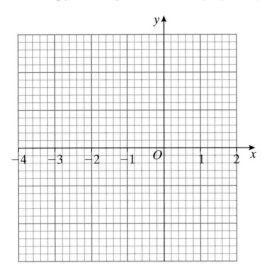

(Total 3 marks)

4 a) On a copy of the grid, draw the line $x + y - 2 = 0$ **(1)**

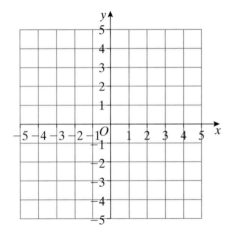

b) Write down the equation of a line parallel to the line $x + y - 2 = 0$ **(1)**

(Total 2 marks)

5   A ramp rises 80 cm in a horizontal distance of 280 cm.

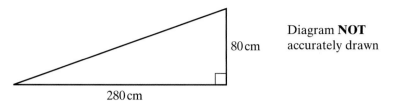

80 cm   Diagram **NOT**
accurately drawn

280 cm

Work out the gradient of the ramp.

(Total 2 marks)

6   The straight line, **L**, passes through the points $(0, -2)$ and $(3, 4)$.

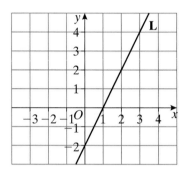

a)   Work out the gradient of **L**.   **(2)**
b)   Write down the equation of **L**.   **(2)**

(Total 4 marks)

7   The total monthly charge for Toni's phone is made up of a fixed fee for line rental plus the cost of the calls. The total monthly charge, £y, for a total of x minutes of calls can be found using the graph below for $x \leqslant 120$, using the straight line **L** on the grid.

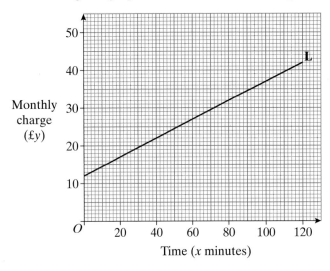

a) i) Find the gradient of the line **L**.
    ii) Give an interpretation of your gradient.   **(3)**
b) Write down the equation of the line **L**.   **(2)**

Toni is offered a replacement phone with a new tariff. There is no monthly rental but the cost of the calls is £0.40 per minute.
c) Find the total number of minutes of calls for which the monthly charge will be the same for each phone.   **(2)**

                                                                                (Total 7 marks)

8   a) Write down the equation of the line which passes through the point $(0, 9)$ and is parallel to the line whose equation is $y = 8x - 5$ **(2)**
    b) Write down the coordinates of the point of intersection of the two lines whose equations are $y = 5x - 2$ and $y = -5x - 2$ **(1)**

                                                                                (Total 3 marks)

9

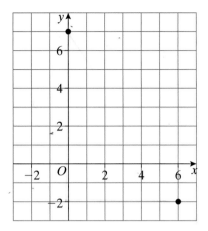

Find the equation of the straight line which passes through the points $(0, 7)$ and $(6, -2)$.

(Total 4 marks)

10 a) Find the gradient of the straight line **L** which passes through the points $(1, 6)$ and $(5, -2)$. **(2)**

b) The line **M** is parallel to line **L** and intersects the y-axis at the point $(0, 1)$. Write down the equation of **M**. **(2)**

c) The point $(3, k)$, where k is an integer, lies on the line **M**. Find the value of k. **(1)**

(Total 5 marks)

11 Find the gradient of the line with equation $y - 3x = 8$

(Total 2 marks)

12 Find the gradient of the line with equation $4y + 3 = 2x$

(Total 2 marks)

13 Find the gradient of the line with equation $3x - 2y = 16$

(Total 3 marks)

14 Integer sequences

1   The table shows the first three terms of a sequence:

Term number	1	2	3		
Term	8	15	24		

The rule for the sequence is

$$\text{term} = (2 + \text{term number})^2 - 1$$

a) Work out the next two terms of this sequence.   **(2)**
b) 9999 is a term in this sequence.
       Find the term number of this term.   **(2)**

(Total 4 marks)

2   Here are the first five terms of a sequence:

     5   11   17   23   29

Find an expression, in terms of n, for the nth term of this sequence.

(Total 2 marks)

3   Here are the first four terms of an arithmetic sequence:

    42   38   34   30

Find an expression, in terms of n, for the nth term of this sequence.

(Total 2 marks)

4   The nth term of a sequence is given by this formula:

$$n\text{th term} = 62 - 5n$$

a) Work out the 8th term of the sequence.   **(1)**
b) Work out the sum of the 8th term and the 9th term of the sequence.   **(2)**
c) Find an expression, in terms of n, for the sum of the nth term and $(n + 1)$th term
       of the sequence. Give your answer in its simplest form.   **(2)**
d) Find the value of n for which $62 - 5n = -23$ **(2)**

(Total 7 marks)

5 Here are the first three terms of an arithmetic sequence:

   $-11 \quad -7 \quad -3$

   The kth term of this sequence is 169
   Find the value of k.

   (Total 4 marks)

6 **a)** Find an expression, in terms of n, for the nth term of the arithmetic sequence:

   $-2 \quad 6 \quad 14 \quad ...$ **(2)**

   b) The nth term of the arithmetic sequence $\quad -2 \quad 6 \quad 14 \quad ...$ is three times the
   nth term of the arithmetic sequence $\quad 151 \quad 152 \quad 153 \quad ...$
   Find the value of n. **(3)**

   (Total 5 marks)

15 Quadratic equations

1 The width of a rectangle is $(x + 2)$ cm. The perimeter of the rectangle is $6(x + 1)$ cm. The area of the rectangle is $18 \, \text{cm}^2$.
Show that $2x^2 + 5x - 16 = 0$

(Total 3 marks)

2 Solve $x^2 - 4x = 0$

(Total 2 marks)

3 Solve $y^2 - 3y - 108 = 0$

(Total 3 marks)

4 Solve $2x^2 - 5x - 3 = 0$

(Total 3 marks)

5 Solve $\dfrac{3(3x - 4)}{x + 2} = x - 2$

(Total 4 marks)

6 Solve the equation $x^2 + 7x + 8 = 0$
Give your answers correct to 3 significant figures.

(Total 3 marks)

7 Solve the equation $5y^2 - 2y - 4 = 0$
Give your answers correct to 3 significant figures.

(Total 3 marks)

8 $y = p^2 + 6p$
Find the values of p when $y = 3$
Give your answers correct to 2 decimal places.

(Total 3 marks)

9 Solve the simultaneous equations

$$y = 2x^2$$
$$y = 3x + 9$$

(Total 6 marks)

10 Solve the simultaneous equations:

$$y = 2x + 3$$
$$x^2 + y^2 = 5$$

(Total 6 marks)

11 Solve the simultaneous equations:

$$2x + y = 1$$
$$x^2 + y^2 = 13$$

(Total 7 marks)

12 Solve the simultaneous equations:

$$x = 2y^2 - 4$$
$$y = \frac{1}{2}x$$

(Total 6 marks)

13 A square has sides of length $(x + 2)$ cm.
A right-angled isosceles triangle has its two equal sides of length $(2x + 1)$ cm.
The area of the square is equal to the area of the triangle.

$(x + 2)$ cm $(2x + 1)$ cm   Diagram **NOT**
accurately drawn

$(2x + 1)$ cm

a) Write down an equation in x.   **(1)**
b) Show that your equation simplifies to $2x^2 - 4x - 7 = 0$.   **(2)**
c) By solving the equation $2x^2 - 4x - 7 = 0$, find the perimeter of the square.
Give your answer correct to 3 significant figures.   **(4)**

(Total 7 marks)

16 Inequalities

1   Solve the inequality $2x + 7 > 13$

(Total 2 marks)

2   Solve the inequality $7x - 3 < 3x + 7$

(Total 3 marks)

3   Solve the inequality $-1 \leqslant x + 1 < 4$

(Total 2 marks)

4   Solve the inequality $-2 < 2x \leqslant 6$

(Total 2 marks)

5   Solve the inequality $0 < 2x + 3 < 7$

(Total 3 marks)

6   **a)**   Solve the inequality $2x + 7 > 1$
    b)   On a copy of the number line, represent the solution to part **a)**.

(Total 4 marks)

7   **a)**   Solve the inequality $2x + 5 \leqslant 11$
    b)   On a copy of the number line, represent the solution to part **a)**.

(Total 4 marks)

8   **a)**   Solve the inequality $-2 \leqslant 4x + 6 < 22$
    b)   On a copy of the number line, represent the solution to part **a)**.

(Total 5 marks)

9 **a)** Solve the inequality $2x + 3 < 13$ **(2)**
   b) n is a positive integer.
     Write down all the values of n which satisfy the inequality $2n + 3 < 13$ **(2)**

                                              (Total 4 marks)

10 **a)** Solve the inequality $4x + 17 > 3$ **(2)**
   b) n is a negative integer.
     Write down all the values of n which satisfy the inequality $4n + 17 > 3$ **(2)**

                                              (Total 4 marks)

11 **a)** Solve the inequality $-4 \leqslant 2x < 3$ **(2)**
   b) n is an integer.
     Write down all the values of n which satisfy the inequality $-4 \leqslant 2n < 3$ **(2)**

                                              (Total 4 marks)

12 Show, by shading on a copy of the grid, the region which satisfies both these inequalities:

     $2 \leqslant x \leqslant 4$ **and** $-3 \leqslant y \leqslant -1$

Label your region **R**.

                                              (Total 3 marks)

13

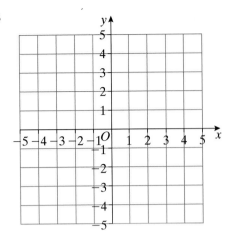

On a copy of the grid, show clearly the region defined by the inequalities:

$$x + y \leqslant 3 \qquad x \geqslant -1 \qquad y > 2$$

(Total 4 marks)

14   Show, by shading on a copy of the grid, the region which satisfies all three of these inequalities:

$$y \leqslant 4 \qquad y \leqslant 4x - 2 \qquad y \geqslant 2x$$

Label your region **R**.

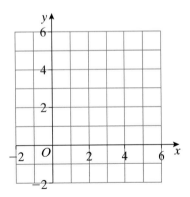

(Total 4 marks)

15 Show, by shading on a copy of the grid, the region which satisfies all three of these inequalities:

$$y \geqslant 1 \qquad y \geqslant -2x \qquad y + 2x \leqslant 4$$

Label your region **R**.

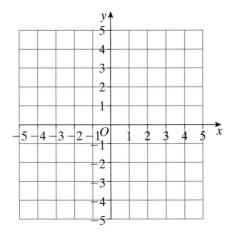

(Total 4 marks)

16 a) Solve the inequality $x^2 < 9$ **(2)**

    b) On a copy of the number line, represent the solution set of $x^2 < 9$

(2)

(Total 4 marks)

17 a) Solve the inequality $x^2 + 1 \geqslant 5$ **(2)**

    b) On a copy of the number line, represent the solution set of $x^2 + 1 \geqslant 5$

(2)

(Total 4 marks)

17 Indices

1 **a)** Simplify $a \times a \times a \times a \times a \times a \times a$ **(1)**

 b) Simplify $p^2 \times p^4 + 3p \times p^5$ **(2)**

 c) Simplify $\dfrac{q^6}{q^2}$ **(1)**

(Total 4 marks)

2 **a)** Work out the value of $2y^3$ when $y = 2$ **(1)**

 b) Simplify:

  i) $c^4 \times c^5$

  ii) $d^6 \div d$ **(2)**

(Total 3 marks)

3 **a)** Work out the value of $x^2 + 5x$ when $x = -3$ **(2)**

 b) Simplify $\dfrac{t^5 \times t^6}{t^7}$ **(1)**

(Total 3 marks)

4 **a)** $F = ab^2 - b^3$

 Work out the value of F when $a = 3$ and $b = -2$ **(2)**

 b) Simplify $p^6 q^2 \times 2pq^3$ **(2)**

 c) Simplify $\dfrac{3r \times (2r)^4}{r^3}$ **(2)**

(Total 6 marks)

5 **a)** Complete a copy of the table of values for $y = x^2 + 2x - 2$

x	-4	-3	-2	-1	0	1	2
y			-2		-2		6

(2)

b) On a copy of the grid, draw the graph of $y = x^2 + 2x - 2$

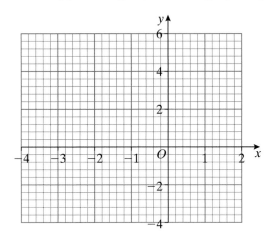

(2)

(Total 4 marks)

---

6 Simplify:

a) $(\sqrt{x})^6$

b) $\dfrac{16y^4}{(2\sqrt{y})^4}$

(Total 3 marks)

---

7 a) Simplify $(3a^4)^3$ (2)

b) Simplify $(8p^9)^{\frac{1}{3}}$ (2)

(Total 4 marks)

---

8 a) Simplify $x^6 \times (x^2)^{-3}$ (2)

b) Simplify $(2p^3q^4)^4$ (2)

c) Simplify $(r^3t^{-4})^{-2}$ (2)

(Total 6 marks)

---

9 Simplify:

a) $(64x^{12})^{\frac{2}{3}}$

b) $\left(\dfrac{x^2}{4}\right)^{-\frac{1}{2}}$

(Total 4 marks)

18 Proportion

1 The extension, E cm, of a spring is directly proportional to the tension, T newtons.
When $T = 14$, $E = 3.5$

   a) Express E in terms of T.   **(3)**

   b) Find the value of E when $T = 10$ **(1)**

   c) Calculate the tension when the extension is 6.5 cm.   **(1)**

                                                (Total 5 marks)

2 The area, A cm^2, of a square is directly proportional to the square of the length, D cm, of its diagonal.
When $D = 7$, $A = 24.5$

   a) **i)** Express A in terms of D.

        ii) On a copy of the axes, sketch the graph of A against D:

                                                (4)

   b) Find the value of A when $D = 13$ **(2)**

   c) The area of a square is 162 cm^2.
       Find the length of its diagonal.   **(3)**

                                                (Total 9 marks)

3 y is directly proportional to the square root of x.
When $x = 16$, $y = 6$

   a) Find an equation connecting y and x.   **(3)**

   b) Find the value of y when $x = 6.25$ **(2)**

   c) Find the value of x when $y = 96$ **(3)**

                                                (Total 8 marks)

4 The mass, M kg, of a solid metal hemisphere is directly proportional to the cube of the radius, r cm, of its circular base.
When $r = 10$, $M = 16$
a) Express M in terms of r. **(3)**
b) The radius of the base of a hemisphere is 7.5 cm.
Calculate its mass. **(2)**
c) The mass of a hemisphere is 250 kg.
Calculate the **diameter** of its circular base. **(3)**

(Total 8 marks)

5 For a fixed mass of gas, the volume, V m^3, varies inversely as the pressure, P newtons/m^2.
When $V = 5$, $P = 200$
a) i) Express V in terms of P.
ii) On a copy of the axes, sketch the graph of V against P:

(4)
b) The pressure of the gas is 500 newtons/m^2.
Calculate its volume. **(2)**
c) Find the pressure of 8 m^3 of the gas. **(3)**

(Total 9 marks)

6

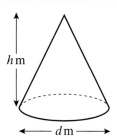

The diameter, d m, of a set of cones, each with the same volume is inversely proportional to the square root of the height, h m.
When $h = 2.56$, $d = 1.5$
a) Express d in terms of h. **(3)**
b) Find d when $h = 10.24$ **(2)**
c) Find h when $d = 3$ **(3)**

(Total 8 marks)

7 The force, F, between two magnets is inversely proportional to the square of the distance, D, between them.
When $D = 4, F = 2$

   a) Find a formula for F in terms of D. **(3)**
   b) Find the value of F when $D = 5$ **(2)**
   c) Find the value of D when $F = 12.5$ **(3)**

                                                  (Total 8 marks)

8 A pebble is dropped from the edge of a cliff.
The edge of the cliff is 250 metres above the sea.
After t seconds, the pebble has fallen a distance x metres.
x is directly proportional to t^2
When $t = 2, x = 19.6$

   a) Find an equation connecting x and t. **(3)**
   b) Find the value of x when $t = 5$ **(2)**
   c) Find how long the pebble takes to fall the final 73.6 m before landing in the sea. **(4)**

                                                  (Total 9 marks)

19 Function notation

1 The function f is defined as $f(x) = \dfrac{x+1}{2}$

   a) Find $f(7)$ **(1)**

   b) Solve $f^{-1}(x) = 2$ **(2)**

                                                                      (Total 3 marks)

2 $f(x) = 4 - 3x$

        $g(x) = x + 1$

   a) Find $fg(x)$ **(2)**

   b) Find $gf(x)$ **(2)**

                                                                       (Total 4 marks)

3 $f : x \mapsto \dfrac{3}{x+2}, \; x \neq -2$

   Find the inverse function f^{-1} in the form: $f^{-1} : x \mapsto \ldots$

                                                                          (Total 3 marks)

4 The functions f and g are defined as follows:

      $f(x) = \dfrac{2}{x+4}$

      $g(x) = \sqrt{x+5}$

   Calculate $fg(11)$

                                                                          (Total 3 marks)

5 The diagram shows part of the graph of $y = f(x)$.

   Use the graph to:

   a) find $f(2)$

   b) solve $f(x) = 2$

   c) find $ff(0.5)$

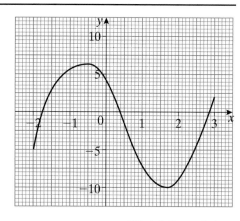

                                                                          (Total 5 marks)

6 f and g are functions:

$$f : x \mapsto 4x - 1$$

$$g : x \mapsto \sqrt{(x + 1)}$$

a) Calculate f(-2) (2)
b) Given that f(a) = 5, find the value of a. (2)
c) Calculate gf(9) (2)
d) Which values of x cannot be included in the domain of g? (1)
e) Find the inverse function g^{-1} in the form $g^{-1} : x \mapsto \ldots$ (3)

(Total 10 marks)

7 The function f is defined as $f(x) = \dfrac{x + 3}{x - 1}$

a) Find the value of:
  i) f(5)
  ii) f($\frac{1}{2}$) (2)
b) State which value(s) of x must be excluded from the domain of f. (1)
c) i) Find ff(x). Give your answer in its simplest form.
  ii) What does your answer to **c i)** show about the function f? (4)

(Total 7 marks)

8 $f(x) = 3 - 2x$

   $g(x) = x^2$

Solve the equation $f^{-1}(x) = gf(x)$

(Total 6 marks)

9 $f : x \mapsto 4x - 3$

   $g : x \mapsto \dfrac{4}{x}, \ x \neq 0$

a) Find the value of:
  i) f(0)
  ii) fg(16) (2)
b) Express the inverse function f^{-1} in the form $f^{-1} : x \mapsto \ldots$ (2)
c) i) Express the composite function gf in the form $gf : x \mapsto \ldots$
  ii) Which value of x must be excluded from the domain of gf? (2)

(Total 6 marks)

20 Harder graphs

1 **a)** Complete a copy of the table of values for $y = x^3 + 3x^2 - 3$

x	-4	-3	-2	-1	0	1	2
y		-3					

(2)

b) On a copy of the grid, draw the graph of $y = x^3 + 3x^2 - 3$

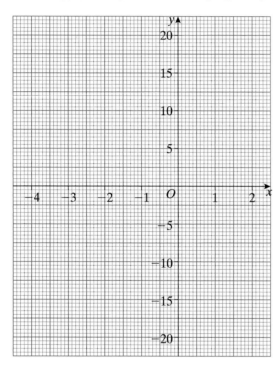

(2)

c) Use your graph to find estimates, correct to 1 decimal place where appropriate, for the solutions of:

i) $x^3 + 3x^2 - 3 = 0$
ii) $x^3 + 3x^2 - 4 = 0$

(4)

(Total 8 marks)

2 Part of the graph of $y = 6 - 2x - x^2$ is shown on the grid.

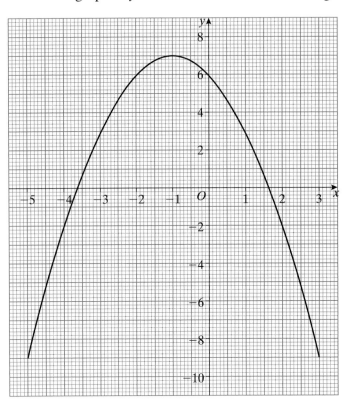

a) Write down the coordinates of the maximum point of the curve. **(1)**

b) Use the graph to find estimates of the solutions to the equation
$6 - 2x - x^2 = 0$
Give your answers correct to 1 decimal place. **(2)**

c) Draw a suitable straight line on the grid to find estimates of the solutions of the
equation $x^2 + 3x - 3 = 0$ **(3)**

(Total 6 marks)

3 **a)** Complete a copy of the table of values for $y = x + \dfrac{4}{x}$

x	0.4	0.6	0.8	1	1.5	2	3	4	5	6
y		7.3		5	4.2		4.3		5.8	6.7

(2)

b) On a copy of the grid, draw the graph of $y = x + \dfrac{4}{x}$ for $0.4 \leqslant x \leqslant 6$

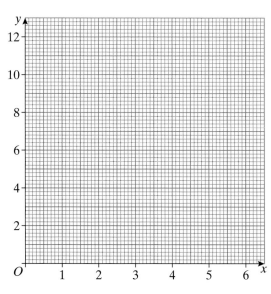

(2)

c) Use your graph to find estimates for the solutions of the equation

$$x + \frac{4}{x} = 6$$

(2)

The solutions of the equation $3x + \dfrac{4}{x} = 10$ are the x-coordinates of the points of

intersection of the graph $y = x + \dfrac{4}{x}$ and a straight line **L**.

d) Find the equation of **L**.

(2)

(Total 8 marks)

4 Part of the graph of $y = x^3 - 4x$ is shown on the grid.

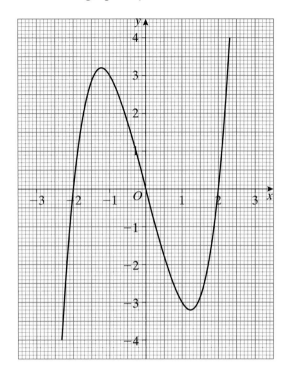

The graph of $y = x^3 - 4x$ and the line with equation $y = k$, where k is an integer, have three points of intersection.

a) Find the least possible value of the integer k. **(1)**

b) By drawing a suitable straight line on the grid, find estimates of the solutions of the equation $x^3 - 3x + 1 = 0$

Give your answers correct to 1 decimal place. **(4)**

(Total 5 marks)

5   The diagram shows part of the graph of $y = f(x)$:

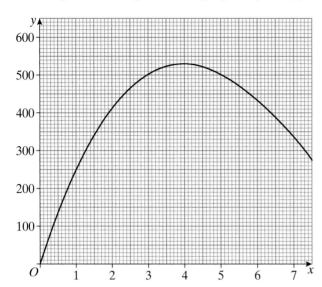

Find an estimate for the gradient of the curve at the point where $x = 2$

(Total 3 marks)

6   On a copy of the grid, draw the graph of $y = 10 + 10x + \dfrac{480}{x^2}$ for $1 \leqslant x \leqslant 7$

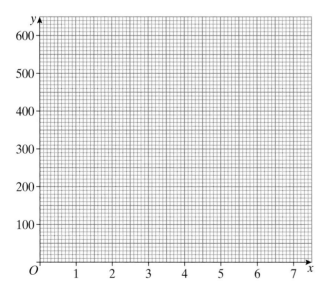

(Total 4 marks)

21 Calculus

1 For the curve $y = 4x^2 - 4x + 1$:

    a) find $\dfrac{dy}{dx}$

    b) find the gradient of the curve at the point where $y = 0$

(Total 6 marks)

---

2 A curve has equation $y = 4x^2 + \dfrac{1}{x}$

The curve has one turning point.

Find $\dfrac{dy}{dx}$ and use your answer to find the coordinates of this turning point.

(Total 4 marks)

---

3 A particle moves along a line.
For $t \geqslant 1$, the distance of the particle from O at time t seconds is x metres, where

$$x = \frac{9}{2t} + t$$

Find the acceleration of the particle when $t = 3$

(Total 4 marks)

---

4 The curve $y = \dfrac{x^2}{3} - 4x + 7$ crosses the y-axis at the point P.

Q is the point $(6, -5)$.

    a) Find the gradient of the line PQ. **(3)**

    b) For the curve, find $\dfrac{dy}{dx}$ **(2)**

The gradient of the curve at point R is equal to the gradient of the line PQ.

    c) Show that R is vertically below the midpoint of the line PQ. **(3)**

(Total 8 marks)

5 A body is moving in a straight line which passes through a fixed point O.
The displacement, x metres, of the body from O at time t seconds is given by

$$x = t^3 + 3t^2 - 9t$$

a) Find an expression for the velocity, v m/s, at time t seconds. **(2)**
b) Find the acceleration when $v = 0$ **(4)**

(Total 6 marks)

---

6 A curve has equation $y = 7 + 6x - 2x^2$
a) For this curve find:

i) $\dfrac{dy}{dx}$

ii) the coordinates of the turning point. **(4)**

b) State, with a reason, whether the turning point is a maximum or a minimum. **(2)**
c) Find the equation of the line of symmetry of the curve

$$y = 7 + 6x - 2x^2$$ **(2)**

(Total 8 marks)

---

7 The diagram shows the graph of $y = x^3 - 3x^2 - 9x + 8$
A is the maximum point on the curve.
B is the minimum point on the curve.

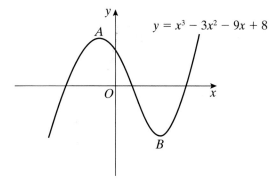

a) For the equation $y = x^3 - 3x^2 - 9x + 8$

i) find $\dfrac{dy}{dx}$

ii) find the x-coordinates of A and B. **(6)**

The line $y = k$, where k is a number, is a tangent to the curve $y = x^3 - 3x^2 - 9x + 8$

b) Find the two possible values of k. **(2)**

(Total 8 marks)

8 The owner of 40 apartments knows that, at a rent of \$360 per week, all apartments will be occupied. For each increase in rent of \$30 per week, one fewer apartment will be occupied.

He increases the rent from \$360 per week to \$$(360 + 30x)$ per week.

After this increase, the total income he receives in rent is \$$R$ per week.

a) Show that $R = 14\,400 + 840x - 30x^2$ **(3)**

b) Find $\dfrac{\mathrm{d}R}{\mathrm{d}x}$ **(2)**

c) What weekly rent should he charge in order to achieve the maximum income? **(3)**

(Total 8 marks)

---

9 A curve has equation $y = x^3 + 75x - 100$

a) For the curve, find $\dfrac{\mathrm{d}y}{\mathrm{d}x}$ **(2)**

b) Find the coordinates of the points on the curve where the gradient is 87 **(3)**

c) Use your answer to part **a)** to determine the number of turning points the curve has. **(2)**

(Total 7 marks)

---

10 The length of a cuboid is twice its width:

2x cm

The volume of the cuboid is 72 cm³.
The surface area of the cuboid is A cm².

a) Show that $A = 4x^2 + \dfrac{216}{x}$ **(3)**

b) Find $\dfrac{\mathrm{d}A}{\mathrm{d}x}$ **(2)**

c) Find the height of the cuboid for which A is a minimum. **(3)**

(Total 8 marks)

Shape, Space and Measures

22 Average speed

1 Rajesh cycled 60 km in 2 hours 30 minutes.
Work out his average speed in km/h.

(Total 3 marks)

2 Sita drove 57 km in 45 minutes.
Work out her average speed in km/h.

(Total 3 marks)

3 Ben ran 100 metres at an average speed of 8.6 m/s.
Work out his time.
Give your answer correct to 2 decimal places.

(Total 3 marks)

4 Preety drove 108 km at an average speed of 45 km/h.
Work out the time it took her.
Give your answer in hours and minutes.

(Total 3 marks)

5 Ali walked for 3 hours 40 minutes at an average speed of 5.4 km/h.
Work out the distance he walked.

(Total 3 marks)

6 Jasmin flew from Dubai to Hong Kong.
Her flight covered a distance of 6052 km.
The flight time was 8 hours 30 minutes.
Work out the average speed for the flight.

(Total 3 marks)

7 Lee flew from Nairobi to Cairo.
The flight time was 4 hours 50 minutes.
The average speed was 738 km/h.
Work out the distance from Nairobi to Cairo.

(Total 3 marks)

8 Tara flew from Amsterdam to Kuala Lumpur.
Her flight covered a distance of 10 430 km.
The average speed was 840 km/h.
Work out the flight time.
Give your answer in hours and minutes.

(Total 3 marks)

9 A snail moves 90 cm in $2\frac{1}{2}$ minutes.
Work out its average speed.
Give your answer in m/s.

(Total 3 marks)

10 The distance between Delhi and Mumbai is 1411 km.
A train covers this distance at an average speed of 85 km/h.
Work out the time it takes.
Give your answer in hours and minutes.

(Total 3 marks)

23 Construction

1   The length of each side of a rhombus is 4.6 cm.
The length of its longer diagonal is 8.4 cm.
Use ruler and compasses to construct an accurate, full-size drawing of the rhombus.
You must show all construction lines.

(Total 3 marks)

2   In triangle ABC, $AB = 6.1$ cm, $AC = 6.9$ cm and $BC = 5.4$ cm.
Use ruler and compasses to construct:
a)   an accurate, full-size drawing of the triangle,
b)   the bisector of angle BAC.
You must show all construction lines.

(Total 4 marks)

3   In triangle PQR, $PQ = 5.6$ cm, $PR = 6.3$ cm and angle $QPR = 58°$.
a)   Make an accurate full-size drawing of triangle PQR.   **(2)**
b)   Use ruler and compasses to construct the perpendicular bisector of the side QR.
You must show all construction lines.   **(2)**

(Total 4 marks)

4   The lengths of two of the sides of a parallelogram are 6.7 cm and 4.6 cm.
The length of its shorter diagonal is 5.1 cm.
a)   Use ruler and compasses to construct an accurate, full-size drawing of the parallelogram.   **(3)**
b)   Use ruler and compasses to construct the perpendicular bisector of the longer diagonal.
You must show all construction lines.   **(2)**

(Total 5 marks)

5   A ladder is 4.8 m long. The ladder leans against a vertical wall with the foot of the ladder resting on horizontal ground.
The ladder reaches up the wall a distance of 4.3 m.
Using a scale of 1 : 50, make an accurate scale drawing and from it find:
a)   the distance of the ladder from the bottom of the wall
b)   the angle the ladder makes with the ground.

(Total 3 marks)

6

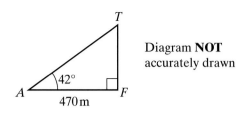

Diagram **NOT** accurately drawn

The Menara tower is in Kuala Lumpur, Malaysia.
F is the foot of the tower and *T* is the top of the tower.
A is a point such that *AF* is horizontal and *AF* = 470 m.
From *A*, the angle of elevation of *T* is 42°.
Using a scale of 1 cm to 50 m, make an accurate scale drawing and from it work out the height of the tower.

(Total 3 marks)

7

Diagram **NOT** accurately drawn

From the top of a cliff, the angle of depression of a boat is 31°.
The height of the cliff is 148 m.
Using a scale of 1 cm to 20 m, make an accurate scale drawing and from it work out the distance from the boat to the foot of the cliff.

(Total 3 marks)

8   A ship sails 126 km on a bearing of 058° from a port *P* to a point *A*.
From *A*, the ship sails 154 km on a bearing of 134° to a point *B*.
Using a scale of 1 cm to 20 km, make an accurate scale drawing and from it find:
a)   the distance *PB*,
b)   the bearing on which the ship must sail to return directly from *B* to *P*.

(Total 4 marks)

24 Geometry

1

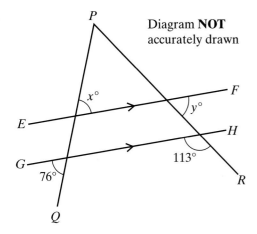

Diagram **NOT** accurately drawn

PQ and *PR* are straight lines.
EF and *GH* are parallel lines.
a) Find the value of *x*.
Give a reason for each step in your working. **(2)**
b) Find the value of *y*.
Give a reason for each step in your working. **(2)**

(Total 4 marks)

2

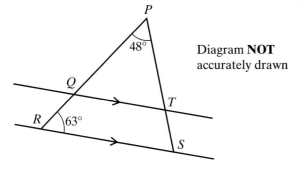

Diagram **NOT** accurately drawn

In the diagram, *PQR* and *PTS* are straight lines.
QT is parallel to *RS*.
Angle *PRS* = 63°
Angle *RPS* = 48°
Work out the size of angle *PTQ*.
Give a reason for each step in your working.

(Total 3 marks)

3

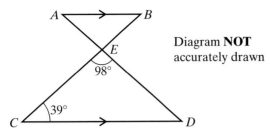

Diagram **NOT** accurately drawn

AB is parallel to *CD*.
AD and *BC* are straight lines which intersect at *E*.
Angle *DCE* = 39°
Angle *CED* = 98°
Work out the size of angle *BAE*.
Give a reason for each step in your working.

(Total 3 marks)

4

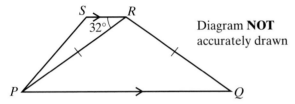

Diagram **NOT** accurately drawn

PQRS is a trapezium. *PQ* is parallel to *SR*.
RP = *RQ*.
Angle *PRS* = 32°
Work out the size of angle *PRQ*.
Give a reason for each step in your working.

(Total 5 marks)

5 **a)** Work out the sum of the interior angles of an octagon. **(2)**
   b) Work out the size of each exterior angle of a **regular** 10-sided polygon. **(2)**

(Total 4 marks)

6 **a)** Work out the size of each interior angle of a regular 9-sided polygon. **(2)**

   b)

Diagram **NOT** accurately drawn

   The diagram shows a regular 9-sided polygon.
   Work out the size of angle *x*. **(3)**

(Total 5 marks)

7 **a)** The sum of the interior angles of a polygon is 1800°.
       Work out how many sides the polygon has. **(2)**
   b) The sizes of four of the exterior angles of a pentagon are 44°, 81°, 109° and 62°.
       Work out the size of the other exterior angle. **(2)**

   (Total 4 marks)

8 The size of each exterior angle of a regular polygon is 20°.
   a) Work out the number of sides the polygon has. **(2)**
   b) Work out the sum of the interior angles of the polygon. **(2)**

   (Total 4 marks)

9 The size of each interior angle of a regular polygon is 156°.
   Work out how many sides the polygon has.

   (Total 3 marks)

10

Diagram **NOT** accurately drawn

Two sides of a regular pentagon, a square and a regular n-sided polygon meet at the point P.
PQ and PR are adjacent sides of the regular n-sided polygon.
Work out the value of n.

   (Total 4 marks)

11

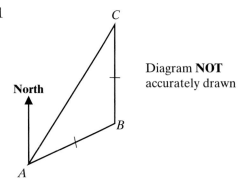

Diagram **NOT** accurately drawn

The bearing of B from A is $076°$

C is due North of B.

$AB = BC$.

a) Work out the bearing of C from A.   **(2)**

b) Work out the bearing of A from C.   **(2)**

(Total 4 marks)

12

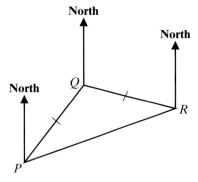

Diagram **NOT** accurately drawn

The bearing of Q from P is $042°$

The bearing of R from P is $067°$

$PQ = QR$.

Work out the bearing of R from Q.

(Total 4 marks)

---

25 Transformations

1

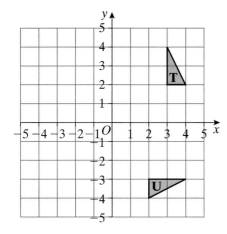

a) Describe fully the single transformation which maps triangle **T** onto triangle **U**. **(3)**
b) On a copy of the grid, reflect triangle **T** in the line $x = 1$
   Label your new triangle **V**. **(2)**

(Total 5 marks)

2

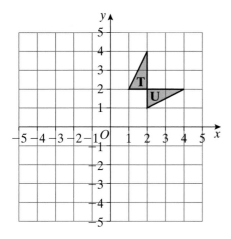

a) Describe fully the single transformation which maps triangle **T** onto triangle **U**. **(2)**

b) On a copy of the grid, translate triangle **T** by the vector $\begin{pmatrix} 1 \\ -6 \end{pmatrix}$
   Label your new triangle **V**. **(2)**

(Total 4 marks)

3

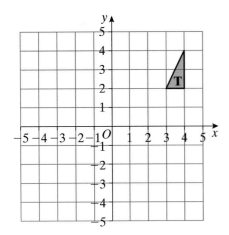

a) On a copy of the grid, rotate triangle **T** through 180° about the point $(1, 0)$.
Label your new triangle **U**. **(3)**

b) On a copy of the grid, reflect triangle **T** in the line $y = 3$
Label your new triangle **V**. **(2)**

(Total 5 marks)

4

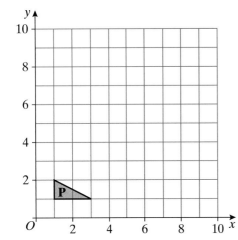

a) On a copy of the grid, rotate triangle **P** through 90° anticlockwise about the point $(2, 7)$.
Label your new triangle **Q**. **(2)**

b) On a copy of the grid, enlarge triangle **P** with scale factor 3 and centre $(0, 0)$.
Label your new triangle **R**. **(2)**

(Total 4 marks)

5

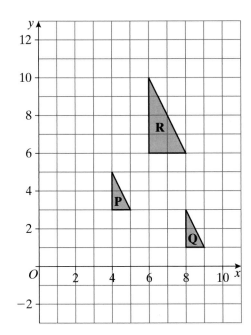

a) Describe fully the single transformation which maps triangle **P** onto triangle **Q**. **(2)**

b) Describe fully the single transformation which maps:
i) triangle **P** onto triangle **R**
ii) triangle **R** onto triangle **P**. **(3)**

(Total 5 marks)

6

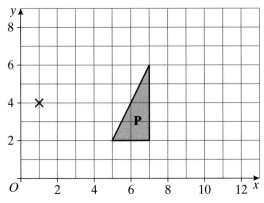

On a copy of the grid, enlarge triangle **P** with scale factor $1\frac{1}{2}$ and centre $(1, 4)$

(Total 3 marks)

7

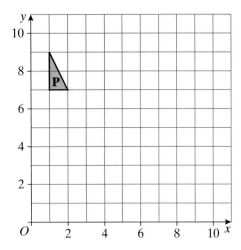

Reflect triangle **P** in the line $y = 6$ to give triangle **Q**.
Reflect triangle **Q** in the line $x = 5$ to give triangle **R**.
Describe fully the single transformation which maps triangle **P** onto triangle **R**.

(Total 4 marks)

8

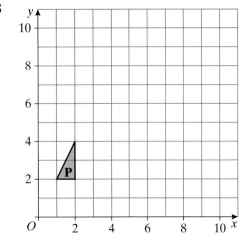

Rotate triangle **P** 90° anticlockwise about $(3, 5)$ to give triangle **Q**.
Rotate triangle **Q** 90° clockwise about $(7, 6)$ to give triangle **R**.
Describe fully the single transformation which maps triangle **P** onto triangle **R**.

(Total 4 marks)

26 Circle properties

1

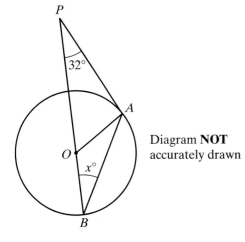

Diagram **NOT** accurately drawn

PA is a tangent at *A* to a circle, centre *O*.
POB is a straight line.
B is a point on the circle.
Angle *APB* = 32°
Find the value of *x*.

(Total 3 marks)

2

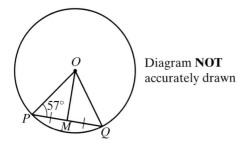

Diagram **NOT** accurately drawn

PQ is a chord of a circle, centre *O*.
M is the midpoint of *PQ*.
Angle *OPQ* = 57°
a) Work out the size of angle *POM*.
b) Give reasons for your answer.

(Total 2 marks)

3

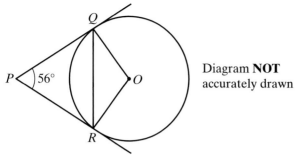

Diagram **NOT** accurately drawn

PQ and PR are tangents to a circle with centre O.
Angle $QPR = 56°$
Calculate the size of angle ORQ.   **(Total 2 marks)**

4

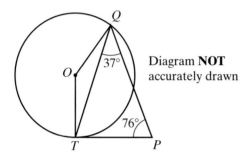

Diagram **NOT** accurately drawn

PT is a tangent at T to a circle, centre O.
Q is a point on the circle.
Angle $PQT = 37°$ and angle $QPT = 76°$
Work out the size of angle QOT.   **(Total 2 marks)**

5

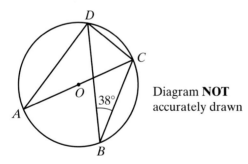

Diagram **NOT** accurately drawn

A, B, C and D are points on the circumference of a circle, centre O.
AC is a diameter of the circle.
Angle $CBD = 38°$
a) i) Find the size of angle DAC.
   ii) Give a reason for your answer.   **(2)**
b) Find the size of angle ACD.   **(2)**
                    (Total 4 marks)

6

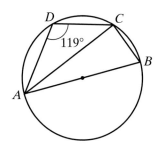

Diagram **NOT** accurately drawn

A, B, C and D are points on a circle.
AB is a diameter of the circle. Angle $ADC = 119°$
a) **i)** Work out the size of angle ABC.
    ii) Give a reason for your answer.   **(2)**
b) Work out the size of angle BAC.   **(2)**

(Total 4 marks)

7

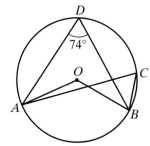

Diagram **NOT** accurately drawn

A, B, C and D are points on the circumference of a circle, centre O.
Angle $ADB = 74°$
a) **i)** Find the size of angle AOB.
    ii) Give a reason for your answer.   **(2)**
b) **i)** Find the size of angle ACB.
    ii) Give a reason for your answer.   **(2)**

(Total 4 marks)

8

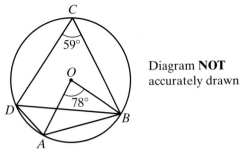

A, B, C and *D* are points on a circle with centre *O*.
Angle *AOB* = 78° and angle *BCD* = 59°
a) i) Calculate the size of angle *ADB*.
   ii) Give a reason for your answer.   **(2)**
b) Calculate the size of angle *DBO*.
   Give a reason for each step in your working.   **(3)**

                                                  (Total 5 marks)

9

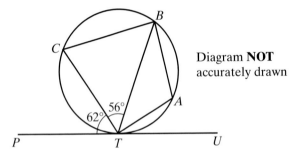

A, B, C and *T* are points on a circle.
PU is a tangent to the circle at *T*.
Angle *PTC* = 62° and angle *BTC* = 56°
a) i) Find the size of angle *CBT*.
   ii) Give a reason for your answer.   **(2)**
b) Find the size of angle *BAT*.   **(2)**
c) Explain why *CB* is parallel to *PU*.   **(1)**

                                                  (Total 5 marks)

10

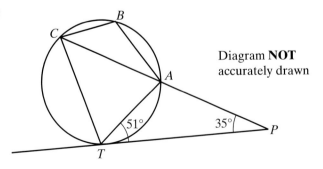

A, B, C and T are points on a circle.
PT is a tangent to the circle at T.
Angle $ATP = 51°$ and angle $APT = 35°$
a) i)   Find the size of angle ACT.
   ii) Give a reason for your answer.   **(2)**
b) Find the size of angle ABC.   **(3)**

(Total 5 marks)

11

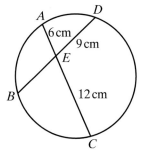

Diagram **NOT**
accurately drawn

A, B, C and D are points on a circle.
The chords AC and BD intersect at E.
$AE = 6$ cm, $CE = 12$ cm and $DE = 9$ cm.
Calculate the length of BE.

(Total 3 marks)

12

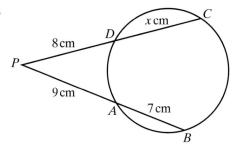

Diagram **NOT**
accurately drawn

A, B, C and D are points on a circle.
PAB and PDC are straight lines.
$PA = 9$ cm, $AB = 7$ cm and $PD = 8$ cm.
Calculate the value of x.

(Total 3 marks)

27 Area and perimeter

1

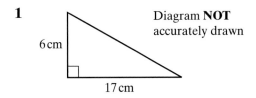

Diagram **NOT** accurately drawn

6 cm

17 cm

Work out the area of the triangle.

(Total 2 marks)

2

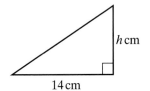

Diagram **NOT** accurately drawn

h cm

14 cm

The area of the triangle is 56 cm².
Work out the value of h.

(Total 2 marks)

3

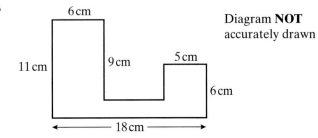

Diagram **NOT** accurately drawn

6 cm

11 cm   9 cm   5 cm

6 cm

18 cm

The diagram shows a shape.
All of its corners are right angles.
Work out the area of the shape.

(Total 4 marks)

4

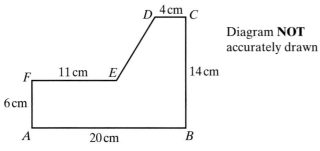

Diagram **NOT** accurately drawn

The diagram shows a shape $ABCDEF$.
The corners at A, B, C and F are right angles.
Work out the area of the shape.

(Total 4 marks)

5

Diagram **NOT** accurately drawn

The lengths of the parallel sides of a trapezium are 13 cm and 7 cm.
The distance between the parallel sides of the trapezium is 8 cm.
Work out the area of the trapezium.

(Total 2 marks)

6

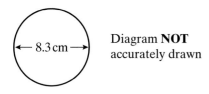

Diagram **NOT** accurately drawn

A circle has a diameter of 8.3 cm.
Work out the circumference of the circle.
Give your answer correct to 3 significant figures.

(Total 2 marks)

7

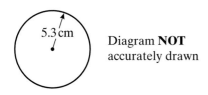

Diagram **NOT** accurately drawn

A circle has a radius of 5.3 cm.
Work out the area of the circle.
Give your answer correct to 3 significant figures.

(Total 2 marks)

8   The circumference of a circle is 23.7 cm.
Work out the radius of the circle.
Give your answer correct to 3 significant figures.

(Total 2 marks)

9

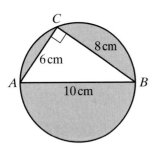

Diagram **NOT**
accurately drawn

The diagram shows a right-angled triangle ABC and a circle.
A, B and C are points on the circle.
AB is a diameter of the circle.
$AB = 10$ cm, $AC = 6$ cm, $BC = 8$ cm.
Work out the area of the shaded part of the circle.
Give your answer correct to 3 significant figures.

(Total 5 marks)

10

Diagram **NOT**
accurately drawn

The diameter of a semicircle is 16 cm.
Work out the perimeter of the semicircle.
Give your answer correct to 3 significant figures.

(Total 4 marks)

11

Diagram **NOT**
accurately drawn

A quarter circle has a radius of 6.5 cm.
Work out the perimeter of the quarter circle.
Give your answer correct to 3 significant figures.

(Total 4 marks)

12

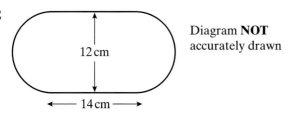

Diagram **NOT** accurately drawn

A shape is made from a rectangle and two semicircles.
The length of the rectangle is 14 cm and its width is 12 cm.
Work out the area of the shape.
Give your answer correct to 3 significant figures.

(Total 4 marks)

13

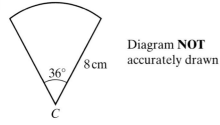

Diagram **NOT** accurately drawn

The diagram shows the sector of a circle, centre C.
The radius of the circle is 8 cm.
The angle at the centre of the circle is 36°
Calculate the area of the sector.
Give your answer correct to 3 significant figures.

(Total 3 marks)

14

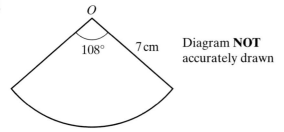

Diagram **NOT** accurately drawn

The diagram shows a sector of a circle with a radius of 7 cm and centre O.
The angle at the centre of the circle is 108°
Calculate the perimeter of this sector.
Give your answer correct to 3 significant figures.

(Total 4 marks)

15 Change 3.7 m² to cm².
Give your answer correct to 3 significant figures.

(Total 2 marks)

28 3-D shapes – volume and surface area

1

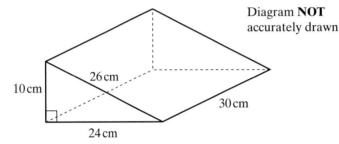

Diagram **NOT** accurately drawn

4 cm
9 cm
7 cm

The diagram shows a cuboid.
Work out the total surface area of the cuboid.   **(Total 3 marks)**

2

Diagram **NOT** accurately drawn

26 cm
10 cm
30 cm
24 cm

The diagram shows a prism.
The cross-section of the prism is a right-angled triangle.
The lengths of the sides of the triangle are 10 cm, 24 cm and 26 cm.
The length of the prism is 30 cm.
a) Work out the volume of the prism.   **(3)**
b) Work out the total surface area of the prism.   **(3)**

(Total 6 marks)

3

7 cm
5 cm
4 cm
5 cm
12 cm
13 cm

Diagram **NOT** accurately drawn

The diagram shows a prism.
The cross-section of the prism is a trapezium.
The lengths of the parallel sides of the trapezium are 13 cm and 7 cm.
The distance between the parallel sides of the trapezium is 4 cm.
The length of each of the other two sides of the trapezium is 5 cm.
The length of the prism is 12 cm.
a) Work out the volume of the prism.   **(3)**
b) Work out the total surface area of the prism.   **(3)**

(Total 6 marks)

4

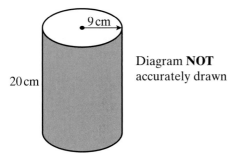

Diagram **NOT** accurately drawn

A solid cylinder has a radius of 9 cm and a height of 20 cm.
a) Work out the volume of the cylinder.
   Give your answer correct to 3 significant figures. **(3)**
b) Work out the total surface area of the cylinder.
   Give your answer correct to 3 significant figures. **(3)**

(Total 6 marks)

5

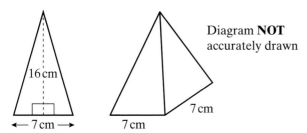

Diagram **NOT** accurately drawn

A solid pyramid has a square base of side 7 cm.
The vertical height of each of its triangular faces is 16 cm.
Work out the total surface area of the pyramid.

(Total 3 marks)

6

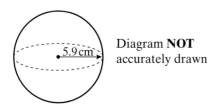

Diagram **NOT** accurately drawn

The diagram shows a solid sphere with a radius of 5.9 cm.
a) Calculate the surface area of the sphere.
   Give your answer correct to 3 significant figures. **(2)**
b) Calculate the volume of the sphere.
   Give your answer correct to 3 significant figures. **(2)**

(Total 4 marks)

7

Diagram **NOT**
accurately drawn

A solid hemisphere has a radius of 4.7 cm.
Calculate the **total** surface area of the hemisphere.
Give your answer correct to 3 significant figures.

(Total 3 marks)

8

5.8 cm

Diagram **NOT**
accurately drawn

9.7 cm

The diagram shows a solid shape made from a cylinder and a hemisphere.
Both the cylinder and the hemisphere have a diameter of 5.8 cm.
The length of the solid is 9.7 cm.
Calculate the volume of the solid.
Give your answer correct to 3 significant figures.

(Total 3 marks)

9   30 cm

26 cm

Diagram **NOT**
accurately drawn

The diagram shows a hemispherical wooden bowl.
The bowl has an external diameter of 30 cm and an internal diameter of 26 cm.
Calculate the volume of wood.
Give your answer correct to 3 significant figures.

(Total 3 marks)

10 The diagram shows a solid cone.
The base radius of the cone is 3.9 cm.
The vertical height of the cone is 5.2 cm.
The slant height of the cone is 6.5 cm.

Diagram **NOT**
accurately drawn

a) Calculate the volume of the cone.
Give your answer correct to 3 significant figures.   **(2)**
b) Calculate the total surface area of the cone.
Give your answer correct to 3 significant figures.   **(2)**

(Total 4 marks)

11 The diagram shows the net of a cone.
Calculate the total surface area of the cone.
Give your answer correct to 3 significant
figures.

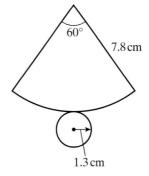

Diagram **NOT**
accurately drawn

(Total 4 marks)

12 The diagram shows the net of a cone.
Calculate the total surface area of
the cone.
Give your answer correct to
3 significant figures.

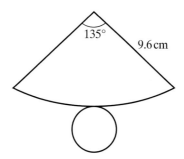

Diagram **NOT**
accurately drawn

(Total 5 marks)

13

Diagram **NOT**
accurately drawn

The diagram shows a solid shape made from a hemisphere and a cone.
The hemisphere has a radius of 4 cm.
The cone has a radius of 4 cm and a slant height of 9 cm.
Calculate the total surface area of the solid.
Give your answer correct to 3 significant figures.

(Total 3 marks)

14

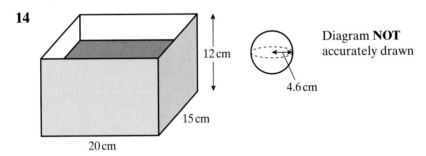

Diagram **NOT**
accurately drawn

A rectangular container is 20 cm long, 15 cm wide and 12 cm high.
The container is filled with water to a depth of 10 cm.
A metal sphere of radius 4.6 cm is dropped into the water and sinks to the bottom.
Calculate the rise in the water level.
Give your answer correct to 3 significant figures.

(Total 5 marks)

15 Change 0.64 m³ to cm³.

(Total 2 marks)

29 Pythagoras' theorem

1

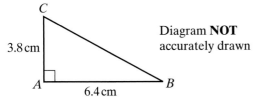

In triangle ABC, angle $A = 90°$, $AB = 6.4$ cm and $AC = 3.8$ cm.
Work out the length of BC.
Give your answer correct to 3 significant figures.

(Total 3 marks)

2

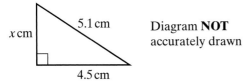

Work out the value of x.

(Total 3 marks)

3

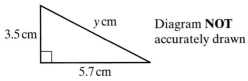

Calculate the value of y.
Give your answer correct to 3 significant figures.

(Total 3 marks)

4

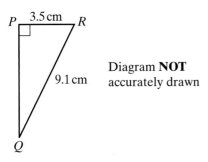

PQR is a right-angled triangle.
$PR = 3.5$ cm and $QR = 9.1$ cm.
Calculate the length of PQ.

(Total 3 marks)

5

Diagram **NOT** accurately drawn

5.2 cm

8.4 cm

A rectangle is 8.4 cm long and 5.2 cm wide.
Calculate the length of a diagonal of the rectangle.
Give your answer correct to 3 significant figures.

(Total 3 marks)

6

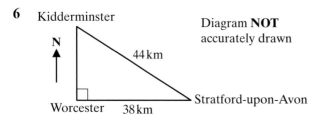

Kidderminster

N

44 km

Worcester   38 km

Stratford-upon-Avon

Diagram **NOT** accurately drawn

Stratford-upon-Avon is 38 km due east of Worcester.
Kidderminster is due north of Worcester.
The distance between Kidderminster and Stratford-upon-Avon is 44 km.
Calculate the distance between Kidderminster and Worcester.
Give your answer in kilometres, correct to 1 decimal place.

(Total 3 marks)

7

A

Diagram **NOT** accurately drawn

6.7 cm   6.7 cm

B   *M*   *C*

⟵ 5.6 cm ⟶

The diagram shows an isosceles triangle *ABC*.
M is the midpoint of *BC*.
$AB = AC = 6.7$ cm and $BC = 5.6$ cm.
Work out the vertical height, *AM*, of the triangle.
Give your answer correct to 3 significant figures.

(Total 3 marks)

8

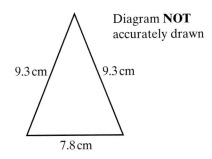

Diagram **NOT**
accurately drawn

9.3 cm   9.3 cm

7.8 cm

The diagram shows an isosceles triangle.
Calculate the area of the triangle.
Give your answer correct to 3 significant figures.

(Total 4 marks)

9

Diagram **NOT**
accurately drawn

6.4 cm   6.4 cm

6.4 cm

The diagram shows an equilateral triangle of side 6.4 cm.
Calculate the area of the triangle.
Give your answer correct to 3 significant figures.

(Total 3 marks)

10 Two points, A and B, are plotted on a centimetre grid.
A has coordinates $(3, 1)$ and B has coordinates $(7, 8)$.
Calculate the length of AB.
Give your answer correct to 3 significant figures.

(Total 4 marks)

11 P is the point with coordinates $(-4, 3)$.
Q is the point with coordinates $(8, -2)$.
Work out the length of PQ.

(Total 4 marks)

12

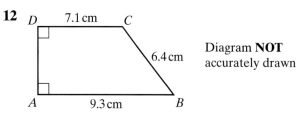

Diagram **NOT** accurately drawn

$ABCD$ is a trapezium, in which AB is parallel to DC.
Angle $A = 90°$ and angle $D = 90°$
$AB = 9.3$ cm. $BC = 6.4$ cm. $CD = 7.1$ cm.
Work out the area of trapezium $ABCD$.
Give your answer correct to 3 significant figures.

(Total 5 marks)

13

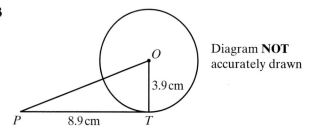

Diagram **NOT** accurately drawn

PT is a tangent at T to a circle, centre O.
a) Write down the size of angle PTO. **(1)**
$PT = 8.9$ cm and $OT = 3.9$ cm.
b) Calculate the length of OP.
    Give your answer correct to 3 significant figures. **(3)**

(Total 4 marks)

14

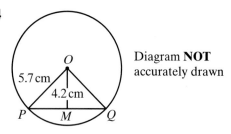

Diagram **NOT** accurately drawn

PQ is a chord of a circle, centre O.
M is the midpoint of PQ.
The radius of the circle is 5.7 cm.
$OM = 4.2$ cm.
Work out the length of the chord PQ.
Give your answer correct to 3 significant figures.

(Total 4 marks)

15

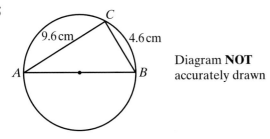

Diagram **NOT**
accurately drawn

A, B and C are points on a circle.
AB is a diameter of the circle.
$AC = 9.6$ cm and $BC = 4.6$ cm.
Calculate the diameter of the circle.
Give your answer correct to 3 significant figures.

(Total 3 marks)

16

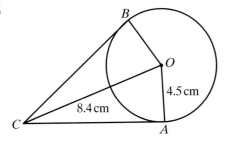

Diagram **NOT**
accurately drawn

A and B are points on a circle, centre O.
The lines CA and CB are tangents to the circle.
$OA = 4.5$ cm and $OC = 8.4$ cm.
Calculate the perimeter of the kite $CAOB$.
Give your answer correct to 3 significant figures.

(Total 5 marks)

17

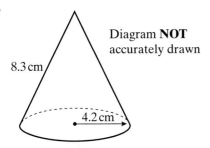

Diagram **NOT**
accurately drawn

The diagram shows a solid cone.
The base radius of the cone is 4.2 cm.
The slant height of the cone is 8.3 cm.
Calculate the volume of the cone.
Give your answer correct to 3 significant figures.

(Total 4 marks)

18

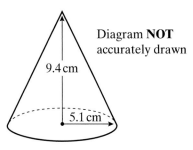

The diagram shows a solid cone.
The base radius of the cone is 5.1 cm.
The vertical height of the cone is 9.4 cm.
Calculate the curved surface area of the cone.
Give your answer correct to 3 significant figures.

(Total 4 marks)

19

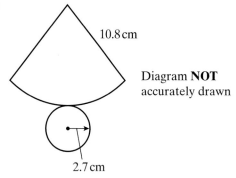

The diagram shows the net of a cone.
Calculate the volume of the cone.
Give your answer correct to 3 significant figures.

(Total 4 marks)

20

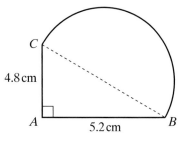

A shape is made from a right-angled triangle, *ABC*, and a semicircle.
In triangle *ABC*, angle *A* = 90°, *AB* = 5.2 cm and *AC* = 4.8 cm.
BC is the diameter of the semicircle.
Calculate the area of the shape.
Give your answer correct to 3 significant figures.

(Total 5 marks)

21

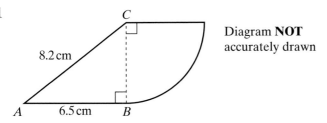

Diagram **NOT**
accurately drawn

A shape is made from a right-angled triangle, ABC, and a quarter circle.
In triangle ABC, angle $B = 90°$, $AB = 6.5$ cm and $AC = 8.2$ cm.
C is the centre of the quarter circle.
Calculate the perimeter of the shape.
Give your answer correct to 3 significant figures.

(Total 5 marks)

22

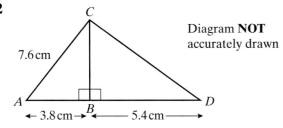

Diagram **NOT**
accurately drawn

Angle $ABC = 90°$ and angle $DBC = 90°$
$AB = 3.8$ cm, $AC = 7.6$ cm and $BD = 5.4$ cm.
Calculate the length of CD.
Give your answer correct to 3 significant figures.

(Total 4 marks)

23

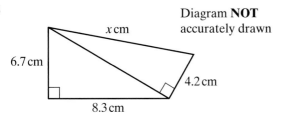

Diagram **NOT**
accurately drawn

The diagram shows two right-angled triangles.
Work out the value of x.
Give your answer correct to 3 significant figures.

(Total 4 marks)

24

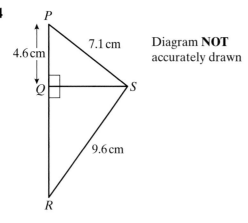

Angle $PQS = 90°$ and angle $RQS = 90°$
$PQ = 4.6$ cm, $PS = 7.1$ cm and $RS = 9.6$ cm.
Calculate the length of QR.
Give your answer correct to 3 significant figures.

(Total 4 marks)

25

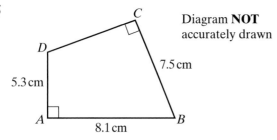

The diagram shows a quadrilateral $ABCD$.
Angle $A = 90°$ and angle $C = 90°$
$AB = 8.1$ cm, $AD = 5.3$ cm and $BC = 7.5$ cm.
Calculate the area of quadrilateral $ABCD$.
Give your answer correct to 3 significant figures.

(Total 5 marks)

30 Trigonometry

1

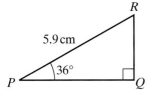

Diagram **NOT**
accurately drawn

The diagram shows triangle PQR.
Angle $PQR = 90°$, $PR = 5.9$ cm and angle $RPQ = 36°$
Work out the length of QR.
Give your answer correct to 3 significant figures.

(Total 3 marks)

2

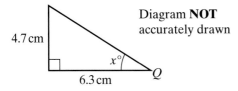

Diagram **NOT**
accurately drawn

Calculate the value of x.
Give your answer correct to 1 decimal place.

(Total 3 marks)

3

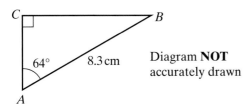

Diagram **NOT**
accurately drawn

Triangle ABC is right-angled at C.
$AB = 8.3$ cm and angle $BAC = 64°$
Calculate the length of AC.
Give your answer correct to 3 significant figures.

(Total 3 marks)

4

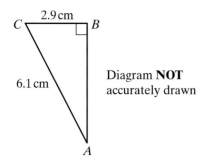

2.9 cm

6.1 cm

Diagram **NOT**
accurately drawn

ABC is a triangle.
Angle *ABC* = 90°, *AC* = 6.1 cm and *BC* = 2.9 cm.
Work out the size of angle *BCA*.
Give your answer correct to 1 decimal place.

(Total 3 marks)

5

7.4 cm

29°

y cm

Diagram **NOT**
accurately drawn

Work out the value of *y*.
Give your answer correct to 3 significant figures.

(Total 3 marks)

6

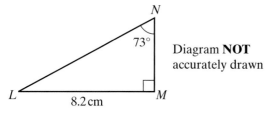

N

73°

L

8.2 cm

M

Diagram **NOT**
accurately drawn

LMN is a right-angled triangle.
LM = 8.2 cm, angle *LMN* = 90° and angle *LNM* = 73°
Calculate the length of *MN*.
Give your answer correct to 3 significant figures.

(Total 3 marks)

7

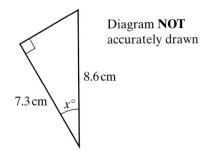

Diagram **NOT**
accurately drawn

8.6 cm

7.3 cm $x°$

Calculate the value of x.
Give your answer correct to 1 decimal place.

(Total 3 marks)

8

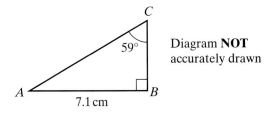

C

59°   Diagram **NOT**
accurately drawn

A

7.1 cm B

Triangle ABC is right-angled at B.
$AB = 7.1$ cm and angle $C = 59°$
Work out the length of AC.
Give your answer correct to 3 significant figures.

(Total 3 marks)

9

Diagram **NOT**
accurately drawn

6.2 m

74°

A ladder is 6.2 m long.
The ladder rests against a vertical wall.
The foot of the ladder rests on horizontal ground.
The ladder makes an angle of 74° with the ground.
Work out how far the foot of the ladder is from the bottom of the wall.
Give your answer correct to 3 significant figures.

(Total 3 marks)

10

Diagram **NOT**
accurately drawn

Stafford is 11 km north of Shrewsbury and 44 km east of Shrewsbury.
Calculate the bearing of Stafford from Shrewsbury.
Give your answer correct to the nearest degree.

(Total 3 marks)

11

750 m   Diagram **NOT**
accurately drawn
23°

An aeroplane climbs for 750 m at an angle of 23° above the horizontal.
Calculate its increase in height.
Give your answer correct to 3 significant figures.

(Total 3 marks)

12

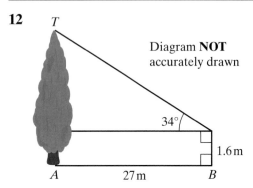

Diagram **NOT**
accurately drawn

Janine is standing on level ground at B, 27 metres away from the foot A of a tree TA.
She measures the angle of elevation of the top of the tree, at a height of 1.6 metres
above the ground, as 34°.
Calculate the height, TA, of the tree.
Give your answer correct to 3 significant figures.

(Total 4 marks)

13

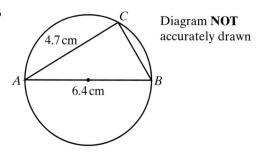

Diagram **NOT** accurately drawn

A, *B* and *C* are points on a circle.
AB is a diameter of the circle.
AB = 6.4 cm and *AC* = 4.7 cm.
Calculate the size of angle *BAC*.
Give your answer correct to 1 decimal place.

(Total 3 marks)

14

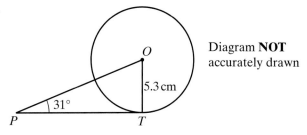

Diagram **NOT** accurately drawn

PT is a tangent at *T* to a circle, centre *O*.
OT = 5.3 cm.
Angle *OPT* = 31°
Work out the length of *OP*.
Give your answer correct to 3 significant figures.

(Total 3 marks)

15

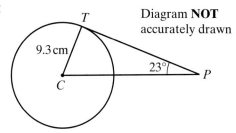

Diagram **NOT** accurately drawn

PT is a tangent at *T* to a circle, centre *C*.
CT = 9.3 cm.
Angle *CPT* = 23°
Calculate the length of the tangent *PT*.
Give your answer correct to 3 significant figures.

(Total 4 marks)

16

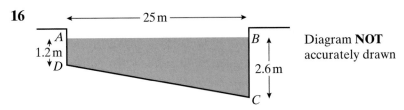

The diagram shows the side view of a swimming pool.
The pool has vertical sides and a sloping bottom.
The water surface, AB, is horizontal and $AB = 25$ m.
The depth of water, AD, at the shallow end is 1.2 m.
The depth of water, BC, at the deep end is 2.6 m.
DC is the sloping bottom of the pool.
Calculate the size of the angle DC makes with the horizontal.
Give your answer correct to 1 decimal place.

(Total 4 marks)

17

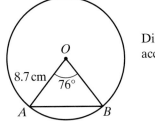

Diagram **NOT**
accurately drawn

AB is a chord of a circle, centre O.
The radius, OA, of the circle is 8.7 cm.
The chord AB subtends an angle of 76° at O.
Work out the length of AB.
Give your answer correct to 3 significant figures.

(Total 4 marks)

18

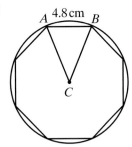

Diagram **NOT**
accurately drawn

The diagram shows a regular octagon inside a circle, centre C.
AB is a side of the octagon and $AB = 4.8$ cm.
Calculate the radius, AC, of the circle.
Give your answer correct to 3 significant figures.

(Total 5 marks)

19

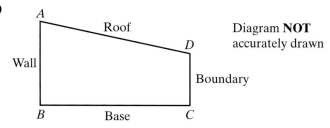

The trapezium $ABCD$ shows one end of a carport.
The base BC is horizontal. AB and CD are vertical.
Carports are made with dimensions in the following ranges:

Wall height (AB)	1.95 m – 2.25 m
Base (BC)	1.80 m – 2.70 m
Boundary height (CD)	1.85 m – 2.10 m

Calculate the size of the greatest angle the roof can make with the horizontal.
Give your answer correct to 1 decimal place.

(Total 5 marks)

20

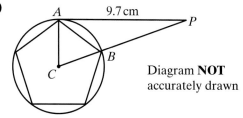

The diagram shows a regular pentagon inside a circle, centre C.
AB is a side of the pentagon.
PA is a tangent at A to the circle.
$AP = 9.7$ cm.
CBP is a straight line.
Calculate the length of AB.
Give your answer correct to 3 significant figures.

(Total 5 marks)

21

The diagram shows two right-angled triangles.
Calculate the value of x.
Give your answer correct to 1 decimal place.

(Total 4 marks)

22

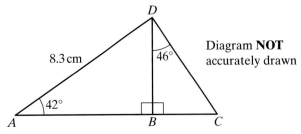

Diagram **NOT** accurately drawn

ABC is a straight line and angle $ABD = 90°$
$AD = 8.3$ cm, angle $BAD = 42°$ and angle $BDC = 46°$
Work out the length of CD.
Give your answer correct to 3 significant figures.

(Total 5 marks)

23

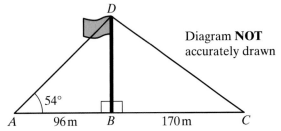

Diagram **NOT** accurately drawn

The diagram shows the Aqaba flagpole in Jordan, which is the tallest flagpole in the world.
The points A, B and C are in a straight line on horizontal ground.
The point B is at the foot of the flagpole and the point D is at the top of the flagpole.
$AB = 96$ m and $BC = 170$ m.
The angle of elevation of D from A is $54°$
Calculate the angle of elevation of D from C.
Give your answer correct to 1 decimal place.

(Total 4 marks)

24

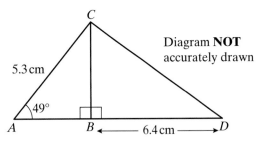

Diagram **NOT** accurately drawn

Angle $ABC = 90°$ and angle $DBC = 90°$
$AC = 5.3$ cm, $BD = 6.4$ cm and angle $BAC = 49°$
Calculate the length of CD.
Give your answer correct to 3 significant figures.

(Total 4 marks)

25

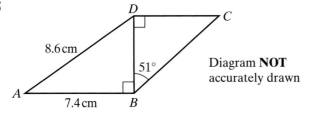

The diagram shows a quadrilateral *ABCD*.
AB = 7.4 cm and *AD* = 8.6 cm.
Angle *ABD* = 90° and angle *BDC* = 90°
Angle *CBD* = 51°
Calculate the length of *BC*.
Give your answer correct to 3 significant figures.

(Total 5 marks)

31 Similar shapes

1 Triangles *ABC* and *DEF* are similar.

Diagram **NOT** accurately drawn

AB = 2 cm   *BC* = 1.8 cm   *DE* = 6 cm   *DF* = 3.6 cm   Angle *DFE* = 76°
a) Find the size of angle *ACB*.   **(1)**
b) Find the length of:
  i)   *EF*
  ii)   *AC*.   **(4)**

                                                                                                                          (Total 5 marks)

2 Triangle *PQR* and *STU* are mathematically similar.

Diagram **NOT** accurately drawn

a) Work out the length of *TU*.   **(2)**
The area of triangle *PQR* is 6 cm².
b) Work out the area of triangle *STU*.   **(2)**

                                                                                                                          (Total 4 marks)

3

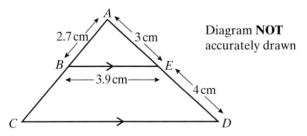

Diagram **NOT** accurately drawn

BE is parallel to *CD*.
AB = 2.7 cm, *AE* = 3 cm, *ED* = 4 cm and *BE* = 3.9 cm.
a) Calculate the length of *CD*.   **(2)**
b) Calculate the length of *BC*.   **(2)**

                                                                                                                          (Total 4 marks)

4

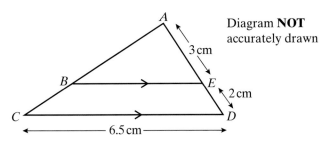

Diagram **NOT** accurately drawn

BE is parallel to CD.
$AE = 3$ cm, $DE = 2$ cm and $CD = 6.5$ cm.
a) Calculate the length of BE. **(2)**
b) The area of triangle ACD is 15 cm². **(2)**
   Calculate the area of triangle ABE.

(Total 4 marks)

5

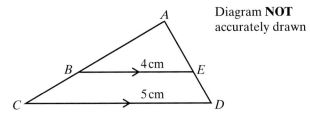

Diagram **NOT** accurately drawn

BE is parallel to CD.
$BE = 4$ cm and $CD = 5$ cm.
a) Find the ratio of the area of triangle ACD to the area of triangle ABE. **(2)**
b) Find the ratio of the area of triangle ABE to the area of trapezium $BCDE$. **(1)**

(Total 3 marks)

6

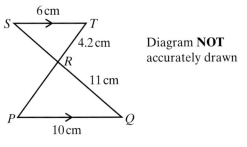

Diagram **NOT** accurately drawn

PQ is parallel to ST.
The lines SQ and PT intersect at R.
$PQ = 10$ cm, $QR = 11$ cm, $RT = 4.2$ cm and $ST = 6$ cm.
a) Calculate the length of PR. **(2)**
b) Calculate the length of RS. **(2)**

(Total 4 marks)

7

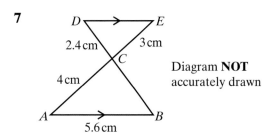

Diagram **NOT** accurately drawn

AB is parallel to *DE*.
The lines *AE* and *BD* intersect at *C*.
AB = 5.6 cm, *AC* = 4 cm, *CD* = 2.4 cm and *CE* = 3 cm.

a) Calculate the length of *BC*. **(2)**
b) Calculate the length of *DE*. **(2)**
c) Find the ratio of the area of triangle *ABC* to the area of triangle *CDE*. **(1)**

(Total 5 marks)

8

Diagram **NOT** accurately drawn

One football pitch is a rectangle 100 m long and 80 m wide.
A second football pitch is a rectangle 110 m long and 90 m wide.
Are the two rectangles mathematically similar?
You must show working to justify your answer.

(Total 3 marks)

9

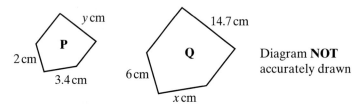

Diagram **NOT** accurately drawn

Pentagons **P** and **Q** are similar.

a) Work out the value of *x*. **(2)**
b) Work out the value of *y*. **(2)**
c) The area of pentagon **P** is 30 cm².
Work out the area of pentagon **Q**. **(2)**

(Total 6 marks)

10

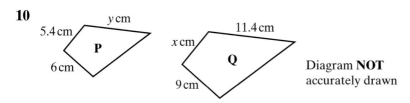

Diagram **NOT** accurately drawn

Quadrilateral **P** is mathematically similar to quadrilateral **Q**.
a) Calculate the value of x.   **(2)**
b) Calculate the value of y.   **(2)**
c) The area of quadrilateral **Q** is 108 cm^2.
    Calculate the area of quadrilateral **P**.   **(2)**

(Total 6 marks)

11

  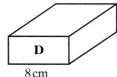

Diagram **NOT** accurately drawn

Two cuboids, **C** and **D**, are mathematically similar.
a) The total surface area of cuboid **C** is 198 cm^2.
    Calculate the total surface area of cuboid **D**.   **(2)**
b) The volume of cuboid **D** is 384 cm^3.
    Calculate the volume of cuboid **C**.   **(2)**

(Total 4 marks)

12

Diagram **NOT** accurately drawn

Cylinders **P** and **Q** are similar.
The total surface area of cylinder **Q** is 25 times the total surface area of cylinder **P**.
a) The height of cylinder **P** is 3 cm.
    Calculate the height of cylinder **Q**.   **(2)**
b) The volume of cylinder **P** is 14 cm^3.
    Calculate the volume of cylinder **Q**.   **(2)**

(Total 4 marks)

13

Diagram **NOT**
accurately drawn

12 cm

x cm

P and **Q** are square-based pyramids.
Pyramid **P** is mathematically similar to pyramid **Q**.
The volume of pyramid **P** is 384 cm³.
The volume of pyramid **Q** is 1296 cm³.

a) The base of pyramid **P** is a square of side 12 cm.
The base of pyramid **Q** is a square of side *x* cm.
Calculate the value of *x*.   **(3)**

b) The total surface area of pyramid **P** is 444 cm².
Calculate the total surface area of pyramid **Q**.   **(2)**

(Total 5 marks)

14

Diagram **NOT**
accurately drawn

10.8 cm

Prisms **S** and **T** are mathematically similar.
The total surface area of prism **S** is 175 cm².
The total surface area of prism **T** is 252 cm².

a) The length of prism **T** is 10.8 cm.
Calculate the length of prism **S**.   **(3)**

b) The volume of prism **S** is 125 cm³.
Calculate the volume of prism **T**.   **(2)**

(Total 5 marks)

15

7.1 cm

8.2 cm

3.7 cm

P

Diagram **NOT**
accurately drawn

A solid shape **P** is made from a cylinder and a cone.
Both the cylinder and the cone have a radius of 3.7 cm.
The length of the cylinder is 7.1 cm.
The slant height of the cone is 8.2 cm.
a) Calculate the **total** surface area of solid **P**.
    Give your answer correct to 3 significant figures. **(3)**

A larger solid shape **Q** is mathematically similar to shape **P**.
The **volume** of solid **Q** is 64 times the volume of solid **P**.
b) Calculate the total surface area of solid **Q**.
    Give your answer correct to 3 significant figures. **(3)**

(Total 6 marks)

32 Advanced trigonometry

1

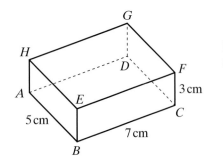

Diagram **NOT** accurately drawn

ABCDEFGH is a cuboid of length 7 cm, width 5 cm and height 3 cm.
a) Calculate the size of the angle that *AF* makes with the plane *ABCD*.
Give your answer correct to 1 decimal place. **(4)**
b) Calculate the length of *AF*.
Give your answer correct to 3 significant figures. **(2)**

(Total 6 marks)

2

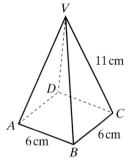

Diagram **NOT** accurately drawn

The diagram shows a solid pyramid.
The base, *ABCD*, is a horizontal square of side 6 cm.
The vertex, *V*, is vertically above the midpoint of the base.
The length of each sloping edge is 11 cm.
Calculate the size of the angle the edge *VC* makes with the base.
Give your answer correct to 1 decimal place.

(Total 5 marks)

3

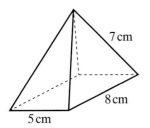

Diagram **NOT**
accurately drawn

The diagram shows a pyramid.
The base is a horizontal rectangle of length 8 cm and width 5 cm.
The vertex is vertically above the midpoint of the base.
The length of each sloping edge is 7 cm.
Calculate the volume of the pyramid.
Give your answer correct to 3 significant figures.

(Total 6 marks)

4

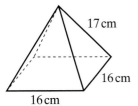

Diagram **NOT**
accurately drawn

The diagram shows a solid pyramid.
The base is a horizontal square of side 16 cm.
The vertex is vertically above the midpoint of the base.
The length of each sloping edge is 17 cm.
Calculate the total surface area of the pyramid.

(Total 6 marks)

5

Diagram **NOT**
accurately drawn

$ABCD$ is a horizontal rectangular field.
AT is a vertical tree.
$BC = 35$ m and $BT = 62$ m.
The angle of elevation of T from B is $16°$
Calculate the angle of elevation of T from C.
Give your answer correct to 1 decimal place.

(Total 6 marks)

6

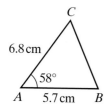

Diagram **NOT**
accurately drawn

In triangle ABC, $AB = 5.7$ cm, $AC = 6.8$ cm and angle $BAC = 58°$

a) Calculate the area of the triangle.
Give your answer correct to 3 significant figures.   **(2)**

b) Calculate the length of BC.
Give your answer correct to 3 significant figures.   **(3)**

(Total 5 marks)

7

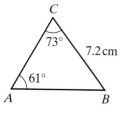

Diagram **NOT**
accurately drawn

In triangle ABC, $BC = 7.2$ cm, angle $BAC = 61°$ and angle $ACB = 73°$
Calculate the length of AB.
Give your answer correct to 3 significant figures.

(Total 3 marks)

8

Diagram **NOT**
accurately drawn

Calculate the value of x.
Give your answer correct to 1 decimal place.

(Total 3 marks)

9 The area of triangle ABC is 17 cm^2.
$AB = 6.9$ cm and $AC = 5.8$ cm.
Calculate the size of the acute angle
BAC.
Give your answer correct to 1 decimal
place.

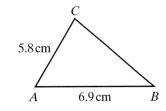

Diagram **NOT**
accurately drawn

(Total 3 marks)

10

Diagram **NOT**
accurately drawn

The lengths of the sides of a triangle are 9.3 cm, 8.1 cm and 5.7 cm.
a) Calculate the size of the largest angle of the triangle.
Give your answer correct to 1 decimal place.   **(3)**
b) Calculate the area of the triangle.
Give your answer correct to 3 significant figures.   **(3)**

(Total 6 marks)

11

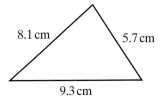

Diagram **NOT**
accurately drawn

Calculate the area of the triangle.
Give your answer correct to 3 significant figures.

(Total 4 marks)

12

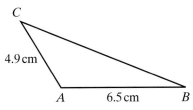

Diagram **NOT**
accurately drawn

The area of triangle ABC is 14 cm^2.
$AB = 6.5$ cm and $AC = 4.9$ cm.
Calculate the size of the **obtuse** angle BAC.
Give your answer correct to 1 decimal place.

(Total 4 marks)

13

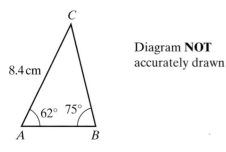

Diagram **NOT**
accurately drawn

$AC = 8.4$ cm, angle $BAC = 62°$ and angle $ABC = 75°$

a) Calculate the length of BC.
Give your answer correct to 3 significant figures. **(3)**

b) Calculate the area of triangle ABC.
Give your answer correct to 3 significant figures. **(3)**

(Total 6 marks)

14

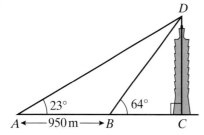

Diagram **NOT**
accurately drawn

The diagram shows the Taipei 101 Tower in Taiwan, which is the tallest building in the world.

The points A, B and C are in a straight line on horizontal ground.

The point C is at the foot of the tower and the point D is at the top of the tower.

$AB = 950$ m.

The angle of elevation of D from A is $23°$

The angle of elevation of D from B is $64°$

Calculate the height of the tower.

Give your answer correct to 3 significant figures.

(Total 5 marks)

15

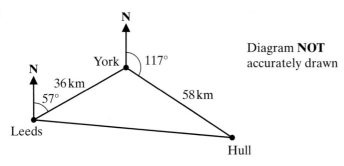

Diagram **NOT** accurately drawn

The diagram shows three cities, Leeds, York and Hull.
The distance between Leeds and York is 36 km.
The distance between York and Hull is 58 km.
The bearing of York from Leeds is 057°
The bearing of Hull from York is 117°
a) Calculate the distance between Leeds and Hull.
Give your answer correct to 3 significant figures. **(4)**
b) Calculate the bearing of Hull from Leeds.
Give your answer correct to the nearest degree. **(3)**

(Total 7 marks)

16

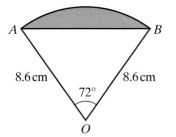

Diagram **NOT** accurately drawn

The diagram shows a sector of a circle, centre O.
AB is a chord of the circle.
$OA = OB = 8.6$ cm and angle $AOB = 72°$
Calculate the area of the shaded segment.
Give your answer correct to 3 significant figures.

(Total 4 marks)

33 Vectors

1   The point A has coordinates $(1, 2)$ and the point B has coordinates $(4, 7)$.

   a) i)   Find $\overrightarrow{AB}$.

      ii)   Find the magnitude of $\overrightarrow{AB}$.   **(3)**

The point C has coordinates $(4, 1)$.

D is a point such that $\overrightarrow{CD} = 2\overrightarrow{AB}$.

   b)   Find the coordinates of the point D.   **(2)**

(Total 5 marks)

---

2 A is the point $(2, 3)$, B is the point $(4, 2)$, C is the point $(5, 7)$ and D is the point $(9, 5)$.

   a) i)   Find $\overrightarrow{AB}$.

      ii)   Find $\overrightarrow{CD}$.

      iii)   Use your answers to parts **i)** and **ii)** to write down two geometric facts about AB and CD.   **(3)**

   b)   Find the magnitude of $\overrightarrow{CD}$.   **(3)**

(Total 6 marks)

3

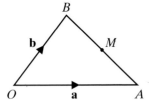

Diagram **NOT**
accurately drawn

In triangle OAB, $\overrightarrow{OA} = \mathbf{a}$ and $\overrightarrow{OB} = \mathbf{b}$.
M is the midpoint of AB.
Find, in terms of $\mathbf{a}$ and $\mathbf{b}$:

   a) $\overrightarrow{AB}$ **b)** $\overrightarrow{AM}$ **c)** $\overrightarrow{OM}$.

(Total 3 marks)

4 *PQR* is a triangle.

X is a point on *PQ* such that $PX = \frac{1}{4}PQ$.

Y is a point on *RQ* such that $RY = \frac{1}{4}RQ$.

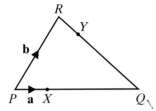

Diagram **NOT** accurately drawn

$\overrightarrow{PX} = \mathbf{a}$ and $\overrightarrow{PR} = \mathbf{b}$.

a) Find, in terms of **a** and **b**:

    i) $\overrightarrow{PQ}$ **ii)** $\overrightarrow{RQ}$ **iii)** $\overrightarrow{PY}$.   **(3)**

b) $\overrightarrow{XY} = k\,\overrightarrow{PR}$

    Find the value of k.   **(2)**

                                                   (Total 5 marks)

5

Diagram **NOT** accurately drawn

PQRS is a parallelogram.

M is the midpoint of *QR*.

$\overrightarrow{PQ} = \mathbf{a}$ and $\overrightarrow{PS} = \mathbf{b}$.

a) Find, in terms of **a** and **b**, an expression for $\overrightarrow{PM}$.   **(1)**

T is the point on *SR* extended such that $SR = RT$.

b) **i)**   Find, in terms of **a** and **b**, an expression for $\overrightarrow{PT}$.

    ii)   Use your answer to part **i)** to prove that P, M and T lie on the same straight line.   **(2)**

                                                   (Total 3 marks)

6

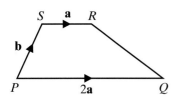

PQRS is a trapezium with *PQ* parallel to *SR*.

$\overrightarrow{SR} = \mathbf{a}$ $\overrightarrow{PQ} = 2\mathbf{a}$ $\overrightarrow{PS} = \mathbf{b}$

M is the midpoint of *PS* and *N* is the midpoint of *QR*.

a) Find, in terms of **a** and **b**:

　　i) $\overrightarrow{RQ}$ **ii)** $\overrightarrow{PN}$.   **(2)**

b) i)   Find $\overrightarrow{MN}$ in terms of **a** and **b**.

　　ii)   Explain what the answer to part **i)** shows about *MN* and *PQ*.   **(3)**

(Total 5 marks)

7

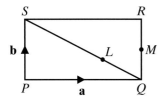

Diagram **NOT** accurately drawn

PQRS is a rectangle.

$\overrightarrow{PQ} = \mathbf{a}$ $\overrightarrow{PS} = \mathbf{b}$

a)   *L* is the point on *SQ* such that $SL = \frac{2}{3}SQ$.
　　Find, in terms of **a** and **b**:

　　i) $\overrightarrow{SQ}$ **ii)** $\overrightarrow{PL}$.   **(2)**

b)   *M* is the midpoint of *QR*.

　　i)   Find $\overrightarrow{PM}$ in terms of **a** and **b**.

　　ii)   Prove that *PLM* is a straight line.   **(2)**

(Total 4 marks)

8

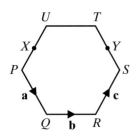

Diagram **NOT** accurately drawn

PQRSTU is a regular hexagon.

$\overrightarrow{PQ} = \mathbf{a}$ $\overrightarrow{QR} = \mathbf{b}$ $\overrightarrow{RS} = \mathbf{c}$

a) Express **c** in terms of **a** and **b**. **(2)**

X is the midpoint of *PU* and *Y* is the midpoint of *ST*.

b) i) Express $\overrightarrow{XY}$ in terms of **a** and **b**.

ii) What does the answer to part **i)** show about *XY* and *UT*? **(3)**

(Total 5 marks)

9

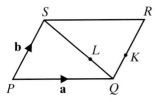

Diagram **NOT**
accurately drawn

PQRS is a parallelogram.

$\overrightarrow{PQ} = \mathbf{a}$ and $\overrightarrow{PS} = \mathbf{b}$.

K is the point on *QR* such that $QK : KR = 1 : 2$

L is the point on *QS* such that $QL : LS = 1 : 3$

a) Find, in terms of **a** and **b**:

i) $\overrightarrow{QS}$ **ii)** $\overrightarrow{PL}$ **iii)** $\overrightarrow{PK}$. **(3)**

b) Prove that *PLK* is a straight line. **(1)**

(Total 4 marks)

10

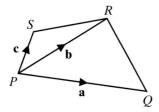

Diagram **NOT**
accurately drawn

PQRS is a quadrilateral.

$\overrightarrow{PQ} = \mathbf{a}$ $\overrightarrow{PR} = \mathbf{b}$ $\overrightarrow{PS} = \mathbf{c}$

D, *E*, *F* and *G* are the midpoints of the sides *PQ*, *QR*, *RS* and *PS* respectively.

a) Find, in terms of **a**, **b** and **c**, expressions for:

i) $\overrightarrow{DE}$ **ii)** $\overrightarrow{GF}$ **(2)**

b) Explain what the answers to part **a)** show about the quadrilateral. **(2)**

(Total 4 marks)

Handling Data

34 Graphical representation of data

1   The cumulative frequency table gives information about the heights of 80 men.

Height (h cm)	Cumulative frequency
$140 < h \leqslant 150$	4
$140 < h \leqslant 160$	14
$140 < h \leqslant 170$	34
$140 < h \leqslant 180$	68
$140 < h \leqslant 190$	80

a)   Work out the number of men with heights in the interval $150 < h \leqslant 160$ **(1)**
b)   Work out the number of men with heights greater than 170 cm.   **(1)**
c)   On a copy of the grid, draw the cumulative frequency graph for the table.

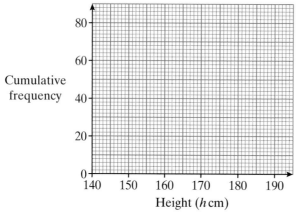

(2)

d)   Use your graph to find an estimate for the number of men with a height of less than 176 cm.   **(2)**

(Total 6 marks)

2 The grouped frequency table gives information about the ages of the 195 members of a sports club.

Age (*t* years)	Frequency
$10 < t \leqslant 20$	20
$20 < t \leqslant 30$	95
$30 < t \leqslant 40$	65
$40 < t \leqslant 50$	10
$50 < t \leqslant 60$	5

a) Copy and complete the cumulative frequency table.

Age (*t* years)	Cumulative frequency
$10 < t \leqslant 20$	
$10 < t \leqslant 30$	
$10 < t \leqslant 40$	
$10 < t \leqslant 50$	
$10 < t \leqslant 60$	

(1)

b) On a copy of the grid, draw the cumulative frequency graph for your table.

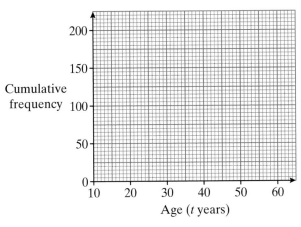

(2)

c) Use your graph to find an estimate for the number of members who are:
   i) aged less than 26
   ii) aged more than 35

(3)

(Total 6 marks)

3 The cumulative frequency graph gives information about the weights, in kilograms, of the sheep in a flock.

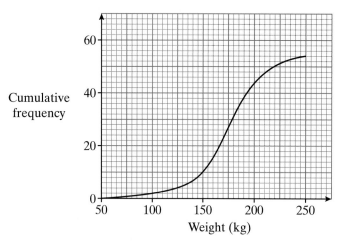

Use the cumulative frequency graph to find:
a) the number of sheep in the flock
b) an estimate for the number of sheep that weighed less than 145 kg
c) an estimate for the number of sheep that weighed more than 210 kg.

(Total 4 marks)

4 The unfinished table and histogram give information about the times taken by some students to complete a homework task.

Time (t minutes)	Frequency
$0 < t \leqslant 15$	30
$15 < t \leqslant 20$	
$20 < t \leqslant 30$	
$30 < t \leqslant 55$	55
$55 < t \leqslant 65$	16

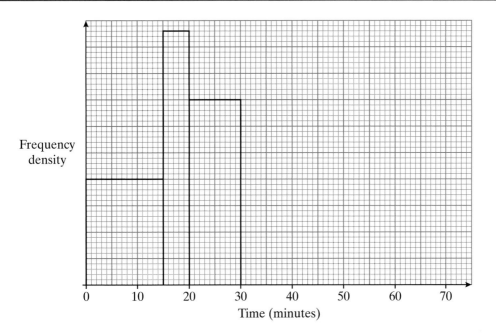

a) Use the information in the table to complete a copy of the histogram. **(2)**
b) Use the information in the histogram to complete a copy of the table. **(2)**

(Total 4 marks)

5 The histogram gives information about the lengths of some pieces of seaweed.

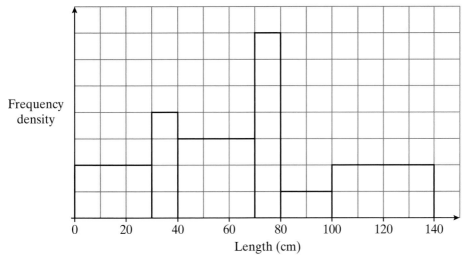

There are 102 pieces of seaweed of length greater than 70 cm.
a) How many pieces of seaweed have a length greater than 1 metre? **(2)**
b) Calculate the total number of pieces of seaweed. **(2)**

(Total 4 marks)

6 The histogram shows information about the masses of some apples.

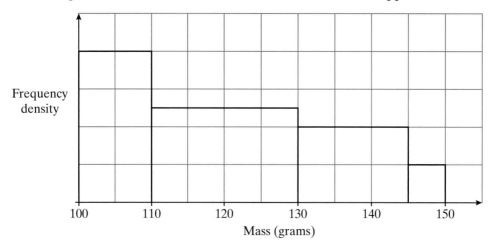

Calculate an estimate for the percentage of these apples that have a mass greater than 140 grams.

(Total 3 marks)

7 The histogram shows information about the heights, h cm, of some Year 12 students.

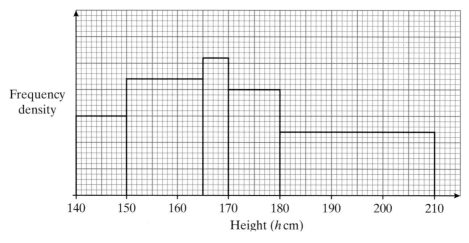

The number of students with heights in the class $170 \leqslant h < 180$ is 20
  a) Find the number of students with heights in the class:
    i) $140 \leqslant h < 150$
    ii) $150 \leqslant h < 165$ **(3)**
  b) Calculate an estimate of the number of these Year 12 students with heights from 175 cm to 190 cm.   **(3)**

(Total 6 marks)

35 Statistical measures

1   The table shows information about the ages, in years, of 20 children at a party:

Age in years	Frequency
3	2
4	12
5	6

a) Work out the range of their ages.
b) Work out the mean age of the children.

(Total 4 marks)

2   The table shows information about the number of empty seats on 40 coaches arriving at a football stadium:

Number of empty seats	Frequency
0	20
1	3
2	8
3	5
4	4

a) Write down the mode of the number of empty seats.
b) Work out the mean number of empty seats per coach.

(Total 4 marks)

3   25 students scored goals for the Year 11 football team last season.
The table shows information about the number of goals they scored:

Number of goals scored	Number of students
1	10
2	4
3	6
4	1
5	4

Work out the total number of goals the team scored last season.

(Total 3 marks)

---

4   Zandile buys 20 boxes of drawing pins. She counts the number of drawing pins in each box. The table shows information about her results:

Number of drawing pins	Frequency
28	4
29	5
30	3
31	8

a) i)   Find the median number of drawing pins.
    ii)   Calculate the mean number of drawing pins in the 20 boxes.   **(5)**
Zandile is given another box containing 30 drawing pins.
b) i)   Without calculating the new mean, state whether the mean will increase or decrease or stay the same.
    ii)   Give a reason for your answer to **b i)**.   **(2)**

(Total 7 marks)

---

5   **a)**   Five numbers have a mean of 8
        Four of the numbers are 2, 7, 9 and 10
        Find the other number.   **(2)**
    b)   Three numbers have a mode of 8 and a mean of 6
        Find the three numbers.   **(2)**
    c)   Find four numbers which have a mode of 4 and a median of 3   **(2)**

(Total 6 marks)

6   A class of 18 boys and 12 girls sit a Science exam.
The mean mark for the boys is 62.5%
The mean mark for the girls is 58.75%
Work out the mean mark for the class.

(Total 3 marks)

7   The mean age of 5 people in a car is 24 years.
The age of the driver is 36 years.
Work out the mean age of the 4 passengers.

(Total 3 marks)

8   The mean height of a group of six boys is 162 cm.
Four of the boys have a mean height of 159 cm.
Work out the mean height of the other two boys in the group.

(Total 4 marks)

9   Adil writes down ten numbers.
The mean of the ten numbers is 17.2
What extra number must Adil write down so that the mean of the eleven numbers is 18?

(Total 3 marks)

10 The grouped frequency table gives information about the daily rainfall in Mathstown
last June:

Daily rainfall (d mm)	Number of days
$0 \leqslant d < 2$	12
$2 \leqslant d < 4$	5
$4 \leqslant d < 6$	6
$6 \leqslant d < 8$	3
$8 \leqslant d < 10$	4

a) Write down the modal class.   **(1)**
b) In which interval does the median lie?   **(1)**
c) Calculate an estimate for the total rainfall last June.   **(3)**

(Total 5 marks)

11 The table gives information about the speeds, in km/h, of 50 cars passing a speed checkpoint on a motorway:

Speed (v km/h)	Frequency
$70 < v \leqslant 80$	4
$80 < v \leqslant 90$	9
$90 < v \leqslant 100$	15
$100 < v \leqslant 110$	16
$110 < v \leqslant 120$	6

a) Write down the modal class. **(1)**
b) Work out an estimate for the probability that the next car passing the speed checkpoint will have a speed of more than 100 km/h. **(2)**
c) Work out an estimate for the mean speed of the 50 cars. **(4)**

(Total 7 marks)

12 The cumulative frequency graph gives information about the time, in hours, spent on the internet last week by each of 80 students:

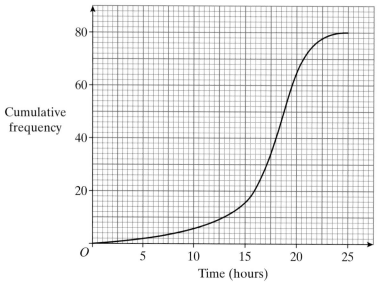

a) Find an estimate for the median of the times. **(2)**
b) Find an estimate for the interquartile range of the times. **(2)**

(Total 4 marks)

13 The table gives information about the number of copies of *The Sunday Headline* sold each Sunday last year:

Number (*n*) of copies sold	Frequency
$20\,000 < n \leqslant 30\,000$	4
$30\,000 < n \leqslant 40\,000$	16
$40\,000 < n \leqslant 50\,000$	16
$50\,000 < n \leqslant 60\,000$	10
$60\,000 < n \leqslant 70\,000$	4
$70\,000 < n \leqslant 80\,000$	2

a) Work out an estimate for the mean number of copies sold each Sunday. **(4)**
b) Copy and complete the cumulative frequency table.

Number (*n*) of copies sold	Cumulative frequency
$20\,000 < n \leqslant 30\,000$	
$20\,000 < n \leqslant 40\,000$	
$20\,000 < n \leqslant 50\,000$	
$20\,000 < n \leqslant 60\,000$	
$20\,000 < n \leqslant 70\,000$	
$20\,000 < n \leqslant 80\,000$	

(1)

c) On a copy of the grid, draw the cumulative frequency graph for your table.

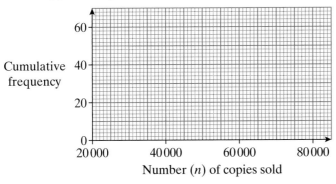

(2)

d) Use your graph to find an estimate for:
i) the median number of copies sold
ii) the interquartile range of the number of copies sold. **(3)**

(Total 10 marks)

14 Here are the ages, in years, of the 11 players in a football team:

   21   26   18   29   20   26   25   19   28   23   21

a) Find
   i) the lower quartile of these ages
   ii) the upper quartile of these ages.   **(3)**

The ages of the 11 players in a cricket team have an interquartile range of 19 years.
b) Make one comparison between the ages of the two teams.   **(1)**

(Total 4 marks)

---

15 All the students in a class took a French test.
There are 15 boys in the class.
The boys gained these marks in the test:

   11   5   14   20   18   4   8   11   18   12   13   15   10   17   7

a) Find the interquartile range of the boys' marks.   **(2)**

In the test, the marks of the girls in the class had a median of 14 and an interquartile range of 6
b) Make two comparisons between the boys' marks and the girls' marks.   **(2)**

(Total 4 marks)

---

16 180 students took an English examination.
The table shows information about their marks:

Mark (x)	Frequency
$0 \leqslant x < 20$	15
$20 \leqslant x < 40$	95
$40 \leqslant x < 60$	45
$60 \leqslant x < 80$	15
$80 \leqslant x < 100$	10

a) Copy and complete the cumulative frequency table.

Mark (x)	Cumulative frequency
$0 \leqslant x < 20$	
$0 \leqslant x < 40$	
$0 \leqslant x < 60$	
$0 \leqslant x < 80$	
$0 \leqslant x < 100$	

(1)

b) On a copy of the grid, draw the cumulative frequency graph for your table.

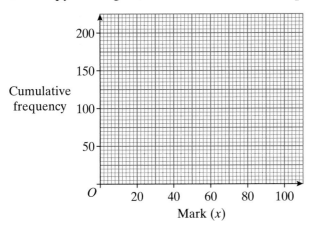

(2)

c) Use your graph to find an estimate for:
   i) the median mark
   ii) the interquartile range of the marks.   **(3)**
d) 145 students passed the examination.
   Use your graph to find an estimate of the pass mark for the examination.   **(2)**

(Total 8 marks)

---

17 The time each of 80 people took to travel to work was recorded.
The lower quartile of their times was 18 minutes.
Their median time was 28 minutes.
The upper quartile of their times was 35 minutes.
Find an estimate for the number of people who
a) took less than 25 minutes
b) took more than 30 minutes.
You may use the grid to find your estimates.

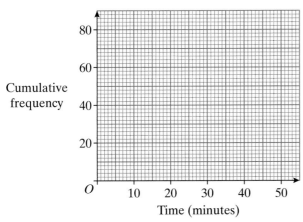

(Total 5 marks)

18 The frequency diagram gives information about the marks gained by a class of 30 students in an examination:

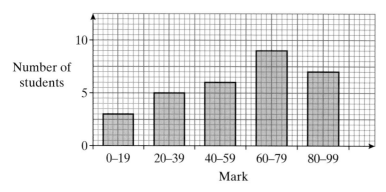

a) Write down the modal class. **(1)**

b) Work out an estimate for the mean mark of the 30 students. **(4)**

c) On a copy of the grid, draw a cumulative frequency graph for the marks.

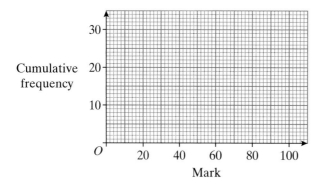

(3)

(Total 8 marks)

36 Probability

1   Cara spins a coin 100 times. It comes down heads 75 times.
   a) Find an estimate of the probability that it will come down heads the next time she
       spins it.   **(1)**
   b) Is the coin fair? Give a reason for your answer.   **(1)**

                                                                    (Total 2 marks)

2   The probability that a person chosen at random is left-handed is 0.1
    350 people are to be chosen at random.
    Work out an estimate for the number of people who will be left-handed.

                                                                    (Total 2 marks)

3   A bag contains red beads, white beads and blue beads.
    Kevin takes a bead at random and replaces it.
    He does this 80 times.
    The table shows the number of times he took a bead of each colour:

Colour	Red	White	Blue
Number of times	19	48	13

    There are 35 beads in the bag.
    Work out an estimate for the number of white beads in the bag.

                                                                    (Total 3 marks)

4   Here is a three-sided spinner.
    Its sides are labelled 1, 2 and 3
    The spinner is biased.
    The probability that the spinner lands on the number 1 is $\frac{3}{8}$
    Mary is going to spin the spinner 48 times.
    Work out an estimate for the number of times the spinner lands on 1

                                                                    (Total 2 marks)

5   Here are ten polygons:

Five of the polygons are squares.
Three of the polygons are pentagons.
Two of the polygons are hexagons.
The polygons are put in a bag.
David takes a polygon at random from the bag 120 times.
He replaces the polygon each time.
Work out an estimate for the number of times he will take:
a) a pentagon
b) a polygon with less than 6 sides.

(Total 4 marks)

---

6   Four athletes Abi, Brendan, Christopher and Dale take part in a race.
The table shows the probabilities that Abi or Brendan or Christopher will win the race:

Abi	Brendan	Christopher	Dale
0.1	0.25	0.3	

a) Work out the probability that Brendan or Christopher will win the race.   **(2)**
b) Work out the probability that Dale will win the race.   **(2)**

(Total 4 marks)

---

7   Here is a four-sided spinner.
The sides of the spinner are labelled 2, 3, 4 and 5
The spinner is biased.
The probability that the spinner will land on each of the
numbers 2, 3 and 4 is given in the table:

Number	2	3	4	5
Probability	0.35	0.15	0.3	

The spinner is spun once.
a) Work out the probability that the spinner lands on 5   **(2)**
b) Work out the probability that the spinner lands on an even number.   **(2)**

Oscar is going to spin the spinner 80 times.
c) Work out an estimate for the number of times the spinner will land on 3   **(2)**

(Total 6 marks)

8 A box contains some shapes.
The colour of each shape is black or green or red or white.
A shape is taken at random from the box.
The table shows the probability that the shape is black or green or red:

Colour	Probability
Black	0.16
Green	0.4
Red	0.2
White	

a) Work out the probability that the shape is white. **(2)**
b) Work out the probability that the shape is black or green. **(2)**

The probability that the shape is a square is 0.7

c) Brody says:
   '*The probability that the shape is a black square is 0.16 + 0.7 = 0.86*'
   Is Brody correct?
   Give a reason for your answer. **(2)**

(Total 6 marks)

9 Ami, Bea, Carla and Deano play a game.
There can only be one winner.
The probability that Ami will win is 0.25
The probability that Bea will win is 0.15

a) Calculate the probability that either Carla or Deano will win. **(2)**

Carla is three times more likely to win than Deano.
b) Calculate the probability that Carla will win. **(2)**

(Total 4 marks)

10 Stuart is going to play one game of tennis and one game of badminton.
The probability that he will win the game of tennis is $\frac{2}{3}$. The probability that he will win the game of badminton is $\frac{3}{5}$

a) Complete a copy of the probability tree diagram to show this information.

b) Work out the probability that Stuart does not win either game. **(2)**
c) Work out the probability that Stuart will win exactly one game. **(3)**

(Total 7 marks)

11 A bag contains 5 black discs and 3 white discs.
Saira takes a disc at random from the bag and notes its colour.
She then replaces the disc in the bag.
Saira takes a second disc at random from the bag and notes its colour.

a) Complete a copy of the probability tree diagram.

First disc　　　　Second disc

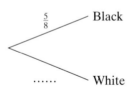

(2)
b) Calculate the probability that Saira takes two white discs. **(2)**
c) Calculate the probability that Saira takes two discs of different colours. **(3)**

(Total 7 marks)

12 In a television quiz show, a contestant must answer one question correctly in the first round to go through to the second round.
In the first round each contestant is asked, at most, two questions.
A contestant who answers the first question correctly goes through to the second round and is not asked a second question.
A contestant who does not answer the first question correctly is asked a second question. If they answer the second question correctly, they go through to the second round. If they do not answer the second question correctly, they are eliminated.
The probability that a contestant will answer a question correctly is 0.6

a) Complete a copy of the probability tree diagram by writing the appropriate probability on each of the four branches.

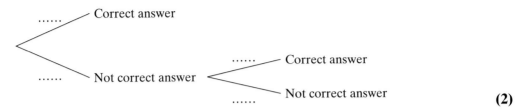

First question   Second question

(2)

b) At the start of the first round, there are 15 contestants.
Work out an estimate for the number of contestants who will go through to the second round. **(5)**

(Total 7 marks)

13 Nick has 10 ties in a bag.
6 of the ties are red and 4 of the ties are black.
Nick takes two ties from the bag at random, **without** replacement.
a) Complete a copy of the probability tree diagram.

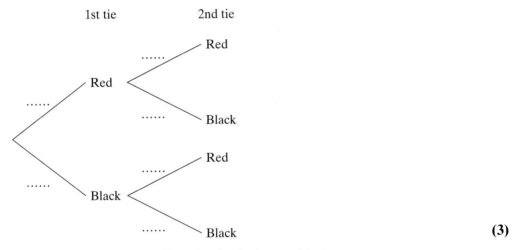

(3)

b) i) Calculate the probability that both ties are black.
ii) Calculate the probability that both ties are different colours. **(4)**

(Total 7 marks)

14

John has six coins in his pocket.
He has one 50 cent coin, three 20 cent coins and two 10 cent coins.
He takes a coin at random from his pocket and records its value.
He then puts the coin back in his pocket.
John takes a second coin at random from his pocket and records its value.

a) Complete a copy of the probability tree diagram.

First coin   Second coin

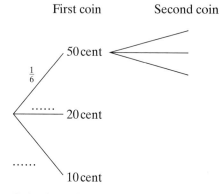

50 cent

$\frac{1}{6}$

...... 20 cent

...... 10 cent
 (3)

b) Calculate the probability that the first coin will be a 20 cent coin and the second coin will be a 10 cent coin. (2)

c) Calculate the probability that the two coins will have the same value. (4)

(Total 9 marks)

15 In order to become a fireman, Adil has to pass a test.
He is allowed only three attempts to pass the test.
The probability that Adil will pass the test at his first attempt is $\frac{3}{8}$
If he fails at his first attempt, the probability that he will pass at his second attempt is $\frac{3}{5}$
If he fails at his second attempt, the probability that he will pass at his third attempt is $\frac{2}{3}$

a) Complete a copy of the probability tree diagram.

1st attempt   2nd attempt   3rd attempt

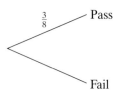

$\frac{3}{8}$ Pass

Fail
 (3)

b) Calculate the probability that Adil will pass the test. (3)

(Total 6 marks)

16 Meg sits a geography test and a biology test.
The probability that she will pass the geography test is $\frac{2}{3}$
The probability that she will pass the biology test is $\frac{5}{8}$
a) Calculate the probability that she will not pass either test. **(2)**
b) Calculate the probability that she will pass exactly one test. **(3)**

(Total 5 marks)

17 The diagram shows eight counters:

Each counter has a letter on it.
Will puts the eight counters into a bag.
He takes a counter at random from the bag and does not replace it.
He then takes a second counter at random from the bag.
a) Calculate the probability that both letters he takes will be L. **(2)**
b) Calculate the probability that at least one of the letters he takes will be A. **(3)**

(Total 5 marks)

18 Here is a biased spinner:

When the spinner is spun, the score is 1 or 3 or 5
The probability that the score is 1 is 0.4
The probability that the score is 3 is 0.5

Kezia spins the spinner twice.
a) Work out the probability that the sum of the two scores is 2 **(2)**
b) Work out the probability that the sum of the two scores is 6 **(3)**

(Total 5 marks)

19 Farah has two bags.
The first bag contains 4 red beads and 1 white bead.
The second bag contains 5 red beads and 3 white beads.

Farah takes one bead at random from each bag.
a) Calculate the probability that Farah takes two white beads. **(2)**
b) Calculate the probability that Farah takes one bead of each colour. **(3)**

(Total 5 marks)

20 A tin of biscuits contains 15 chocolate biscuits and 10 cream biscuits.
Silvia takes a biscuit at random from the tin and eats it.
She then takes another biscuit at random from the tin and eats it.
a) Calculate the probability that both the biscuits Silvia eats are chocolate. **(2)**
b) Calculate the probability that at least one of the biscuits Silvia eats is cream. **(3)**

(Total 5 marks)

21 Harry has a biased coin.
When he spins the coin, the probability that it will come down tails is 0.7
Harry spins the coin three times.
a) Calculate the probability that it comes down **heads** every time. **(2)**
b) Calculate the probability that it comes down tails at least twice. **(4)**

(Total 6 marks)

22 Mandy has 20 stamps in an envelope.
10 stamps are German.
8 stamps are Spanish.
2 stamps are English.
Mandy takes three stamps from the envelope at random, **without** replacement.
a) Calculate the probability that Mandy takes both English stamps. **(3)**
b) Calculate the probability that she takes stamps from at least two countries. **(3)**

(Total 6 marks)

23 A fair six-sided dice has faces numbered 1, 2, 3, 4, 5 and 6
When a dice is thrown the number facing up is the score.
The dice is thrown three times.
Calculate the probability that the total score is 5

(Total 4 marks)

24 A weekend tennis tournament is due to take place next Saturday and Sunday.
If rain interrupts play on the Saturday, the probability that it will interrupt play on the Sunday is 0.75
If rain does not interrupt play on the Saturday, the probability that it will interrupt play on the Sunday is 0.2
The probability that rain will interrupt play on the Saturday is 0.6
a) Calculate the probability that rain will **not** interrupt play during the tournament. **(3)**
b) Calculate the probability that rain will interrupt play on the Sunday. **(3)**

(Total 6 marks)

25 There are n marbles in a bag.
Five of the marbles are green and the rest are yellow.
Alison takes one marble at random from the bag.
She records its colour and then replaces it.
She takes a second marble at random from the bag and records its colour.
The probability that the two marbles Alison takes will have different colours is $\frac{3}{8}$
Show that $3n^2 - 80n + 400 = 0$

(Total 4 marks)

Answers

NUMBER

1 Decimals

1. £46.74
2. a) £14.40 b) i) £56.00
   ii) 3 hours 53 min 20 sec
3. a) £55.63 b) £830
4. £35.36
   1314
   £123.91
   £159.27
   £7.96
   £167.23
5. 4.4
6. 3.5
7. 8.2352941…
8. a) 1.4541019… b) 1.45
9. a) 0.0055555… b) 0.0056
10. a) 8.50121577… b) 8.50
13. $\frac{7}{11}$
16. $\frac{29}{45}$
17. a) for example 63
    b) multiple of 21

2 Powers and roots

1. 5.74569404…
2. a) 1.074172311… b) 1.07
3. a) 17.08016258 b) 17.08
4. a) 5.329668024… b) 5.330
5. $5 \times 5 \times 7$
6. $2^3 \times 7^2$
7. $2^2 \times 3 \times 5^2$
8. a) i) $2^2 \times 3^3$ ii) $2^4 \times 3^2$
   b) 36
9. a) $2 \times 3 \times 5 \times 5$ b) 450
10. a) 21 b) 735
11. a) $(6 + 4) \times 2 = 20$
    b) $6 \div 4 + 2 = 3.5$
    c) $6 \div (4 \times 2) = \frac{3}{4}$
12. a) $\frac{1}{3}$ b) $0.\dot{3}$

13. a) i) 5^{12} ii) 9^3 b) $n = 9$
14. a) i) 4^8 ii) 6^{-2} b) 0
15. a) $\frac{1}{81}$ b) $\frac{4}{7}$ c) $\frac{9}{64}$
16. a) $3^{\frac{3}{2}}$ b) $8^{\frac{1}{6}}$ c) $2^{-\frac{7}{2}}$

3 Fractions

17. $\frac{5}{8}$
18. 12
20. 25
21. $\frac{1}{3}$
22. 14 850 m^3
23. $\frac{2}{3}$
24. 24
25. a) $3000 b) $\frac{2}{3}$

4 Percentages

1. 18%
2. 14%
3. 4%
4. $7905
5. a) £39.60 b) £575
6. £850
7. 175
8. 32%
9. a) 72% b) 140
10. £533
11. 16%
12. £120
13. 6.4%
14. £29 260
15. 12%
16. £180 000
17. 510 000 000 km^2
18. a) 12% b) 115% c) 24 g
19. 9952
20. £1020
21. $156
22. 4.5% per annum
23. 81.6 cm
24. a) £198 b) £520

25. £6615
26. $624.32
27. £8201.25
28. 6
29. £27 500
30. 14
31. 82%
32. 32%
33. No (it's the same as an increase of 4%)
34. 17%
35. Decrease of 28%

5 Ratio and proportion

1. 1 : 0.08
2. 1 : 150
3. a) 1:25 b) 9 m
4. 60 300
5. $336
6. a) 3.25 kg copper,
   1.75 kg zinc b) 650 grams
7. 24.2 cm
8. 105°
9. $18\frac{2}{3}$
10. a) 39 b) $1134
11. a) 180 km b) 6 mm
12. 375 g of pastry, 1125 g of potatoes, 550 g of onions, 800 g of bacon
13. a) £1242 b) €300

6 Standard form

1. a) 2.3×10^5 b) 0.0063
2. a) 4.7×10^{-4} b) 3 700 000
   c) 6.25×10^7
3. a) 5.8×10^7 b) 2.9×10^9 km
4. 4.8×10^2
5. 7.67×10^4
6. a) 1.5×10^{10}
   b) 15 gigayears

7 **a)** 1.67×10^{-24}
  b) 9.0×10^{-28} g
8 1.42×10^8
9 5.8×10^8 km^2
10 5.13×10^{-5}
11 **a)** 1.23×10^{13} **b)** 1.8×10^{17}
  c) 8.1×10^{-5} nanoseconds
12 2.8×10^{-5}
13 2.3×10^6 years
14 7.67×10^{-4}
15 8.3×10^{-3} cm
16 7.1×10^8
17 **a)** 1.992×10^{-26} kg **b)** 197
18 **a)** 4.1×10^{13} km
  b) 2.8×10^4 light years
19 **a)** 0.000 002 2
  b) 2.91×10^{-13} s
20 **a)** 81 **b)** 5.8×10^{20}
21 $6 \times 10^{m+n}$
22 **i)** $2.4 \times 10^{m+n+1}$
  ii) $1.5 \times 10^{m-n}$
23 $4.9 \times 10^{2n+1}$
24 $6.25 \times 10^{m-n-1}$
25 6
26 $a = 9$ $n = -10$
27 $a = 8$ $n = -4$
28 **a)** 5 **b)** -3

7 Degree of accuracy

1 3, 30, 0.4
2 **a)** 40, 9, 30 **b)** 12
  c) Both numbers in the numerator have been rounded down and the number in the denominator has been rounded up.
3 **a)** 40, 80, 0.5, 4 **b)** 1600
  c) Both numbers in the numerator have been rounded up; both numbers in the denominator have been rounded down (and the final rounding was up).
4 **i)** 6.45 kg **ii)** 6.35 kg
5 **i)** 11.85 cm **ii)** 11.75 cm
6 22.6 kg
7 **a) i)** 29.8 cm **ii)** 29.4 cm

  b) i) 30 cm **ii)** Upper and lower bounds agree to 1 significant figure.
8 1077 km
9 **a)** 2 **b)** 61.75
10 4.7 cm
11 0.13 m or 13 cm
12 3
13 **a)** 7.464366831
  b) Lower bound $= \dfrac{23.35}{\pi}$
  $= 7.432535842$ and so upper and lower bounds agree to 1 sf i.e. 7 cm
14 6.210526316 cm
15 842.625 km
16 7.025641026 m/s
17 35
18 14 cm
19 23 (Upper bound $= 23.06805075$ lower bound $= 22.50137724$ so bounds agree to 2 sf)
20 0.8 (Upper bound $= 0.793103448$ lower bound $= 0.768707483$ so bounds agree to 1 sf)

8 Set language and notation

1 **a) i)** 1, 2, 3, 4, 5, 6, 8 **ii)** 1, 3
  b) 5 is not a member of set A.
2 **a) i)** rhombuses, squares, kites
  ii) squares
  b) i) $21 \notin \mathscr{E}$
  ii) No, $14 \in P$ and $14 \in Q$
3 **a)** 3, 4, 6, 8 **b)** eg 1, 2, 5, 7
4 **a) i)** {9, 10, 11, 12, 13}
  ii) {14, 15} **b)** $\varnothing$
5 **a)** 21, 23, 28, 29 **b)** $\varnothing$ **c)** No; 27 is not a prime number
6 **a) i)** $12 \notin \mathscr{E}$ since 12 is not odd.
  ii) 1, 3, 5, 15
  b) 1, 3

7

8 **a)** $A \cap B' = A$
  b) $A' \cup B = \mathscr{E}$
9 **a) i)**

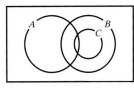

  ii) eg 3, 7 **iii)** eg 5, 15
  b) i)

  ii) 3
10 **a) i)** 5 **ii)** 15 **iii)** 6
  b) i) 25 **ii)** 15 **iii)** 0
11 **a) i)** $13 - x$ **ii)** $10 - x$
  b) 8
12 15

ALGEBRA

9 Algebraic manipulation

1 **a)** $6b - 5a - 1$ **b)** $6p + 21$
  c) $3(3x + 4)$
2 **a)** $3x^2 + 2x$ **b)** $15x + 11$
  c) $y^2 + 6y + 8$
3 **a)** $8x + 11$ **b)** $5x^2 + 4xy$
  c) $4(3y - 2)$
4 **a)** $9y - 13$ **b)** $5(3 - 4p)$
  c) $x^2 - 5x - 6$
5 **a)** $7q^3 + 5q$ **b)** $-3y - 7$
  c) $x(x - 6)$

6 **a)** $11 - 5y$ **b)** $2x^2 - 6xy$

7 **a)** $14x - 21$ **b)** $3p^4 - 3p^3$

c) $y^2 - 6y + 5$

8 **a)** $2x(9 - 4x)$

b) $(x + 4)(x + 5)$

9 **a)** $6p^2 + 11pq - 10q^2$

b) $(x + 4)(x - 4)$

10 $(x + 2)(x - 10)$

11 $(x + 5)(2x - 1)$

12 $2(4x - 3)(x + 2)$

13 $3(2x + 5)(2x - 5)$

14 $\dfrac{x + 2}{4}$

15 $\dfrac{x + 3}{x + 1}$

16 $\dfrac{x - 3}{x - 12}$

17 $\dfrac{x + 2}{x - 2}$

18 $\dfrac{x + 4}{2x - 3}$

19 $\dfrac{5}{x - 3}$

20 $\dfrac{2}{x + 4}$

21 **a)** $(3x + 1)(3x - 1)$

b) i) 29×31

ii) $2 \times 2 \times 5 \times 5 \times 29 \times 31$

10 Expressions and formulae

1 27

2 6

3 4.4

4 4.6

5 $\dfrac{8}{15}$

6 $F = 40H + 32$

7 **a)** 50 **b)** $P = 2(2n+1)$

c) $n = \dfrac{P - 2}{4}$

8 Either $r = +\sqrt{\dfrac{A}{\pi}}$ or

$r = -\sqrt{\dfrac{A}{\pi}}$

9 $h = \dfrac{mx - y}{m}$

10 $s = \dfrac{at^2}{2}$

11 $x = \dfrac{2y - 6b}{3 + 5y}$ or $x = \dfrac{2(y - 3b)}{3 + 5y}$

12 $x = \dfrac{a}{y} - a$

13 Either $r = +\sqrt{\dfrac{aR^2 + t - T}{a}}$

or $r = -\sqrt{\dfrac{aR^2 + t - T}{a}}$

14 **a)** 44 **b)** $P = 4\sqrt{A}$

c) $A = \dfrac{P^2}{16}$

11 Linear equations and simultaneous equations

1 $x = \dfrac{8}{3}$

2 $x = -\dfrac{5}{6}$

3 $y = \dfrac{1}{2}$

4 $x = 12$

5 $x = \dfrac{3}{2}$

6 $x = \dfrac{1}{2}$

7 $x = -\dfrac{3}{8}$

8 $x = \dfrac{1}{2}$

9 $x = \dfrac{9}{5}$

10 $x = \dfrac{1}{10}$

11 $y = \dfrac{11}{5}$

12 $p = -\dfrac{4}{3}$

13 **a)** $6x - 1 = 14$ **b)** $x = \dfrac{5}{2}$

c) 6 cm

14 **a)** $4x + 10 = 2(x + 10)$

b) 5 years

15 **a)** $3x - 8 = 2(x + 8)$ **b)** 84°

16 $x = -\dfrac{1}{2}$

17 $t = 1.4$

18 $a = 1.6$

19 $x = -0.5, y = -4.5$

20 $x = 1.5, y = -1$

21 $x = 3, y = 1.5$

22 **a)** $x = \dfrac{3}{4}, y = -\dfrac{1}{2}$ **b)** $(\frac{3}{4}, -\frac{1}{2})$

23 $(\frac{5}{4}, \frac{1}{2})$

12 Coordinates and graphs

1 $(3, 7)$

2 $(1, 8)$

3 **a)** $(-1, 8)$ **b)** $(1.5, 6.5)$

4 **a)** 1230 **b)** 10 **c)** 100

d) 1210 and 1230

e) 1225, 1250 and 1305

f) 80 km/h

5 **a)** 10 **b)** 12 km **c)** 12 km/h

d) i)

ii) 105

6 **a)** 2.8 m/s² **b) i)** 28 m/s

ii) 504 m

c)

7 **a)** 25 m **b)** 45 m

c) 2 seconds

13 Linear graphs

1 **b)** $(-1, 4)$

2 **b)** $(-2, -3)$

4 **b)** eg $x + y - 3 = 0$.

5 $\dfrac{2}{7}$

6 **a)** 2 **b)** $y = 2x - 2$

7 **a) i)** 0.25 **ii)** Cost, in pounds, of a 1 minute call
b) $y = 0.25x + 12$ **c)** 80

8 **a)** $y = 8x + 9$ **b)** $(0, -2)$

9 $y = -1.5x + 7$

10 **a)** -2 **b)** $y = -2x + 1$
c) -5

11 3

12 0.5

13 1.5

14 Integer sequences

1 **a)** 35, 48 **b)** 98

2 $6n - 1$

3 $46 - 4n$

4 **a)** 22 **b)** 39 **c)** $119 - 10n$
d) 17

5 46

6 **a)** $8n - 10$ **b)** 92

15 Quadratic equations

2 $x = 0, x = 4$

3 $y = -9, y = 12$

4 $x = -\frac{1}{2}, x = 3$

5 $x = 1, x = 8$

6 $x = -5.56, x = -1.44$

7 $y = -0.717, y = 1.12$

8 $p = -6.46, p = 0.46$

9 $x = -\frac{3}{2}, y = \frac{9}{2}$ and $x = 3$, $y = 18$

10 $x = -\frac{2}{5}, y = 2\frac{1}{5}$ and $x = -2$, $y = -1$

11 $x = -1\frac{1}{5}, y = 3\frac{2}{5}$ and $x = 2$, $y = -3$

12 $x = -2, y = -1$ and $x = 4$, $y = 2$

13 **a)** $(x + 2)^2 = \frac{1}{2}(2x + 1)^2$
c) 12.5 cm

16 Inequalities

1 $x > 3$

2 $x < 2.5$

3 $-2 \leqslant x < 3$

4 $-1 < x \leqslant 3$

5 $-1.5 < x < 2$

6 **a)** $x > -3$
b)

7 **a)** $x \leqslant 3$
b)

8 **a)** $-2 \leqslant x < 4$
b)

9 **a)** $x < 5$ **b)** 1, 2, 3, 4

10 **a)** $x > -3.5$ **b)** $-3, -2, -1$

11 **a)** $-2 \leqslant x < 1.5$
b) $-2, -1, 0, 1$

12

13

14

15
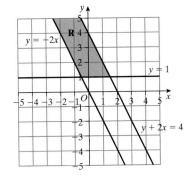

16 **a)** $-3 < x < 3$
b)

17 **a)** $x \leqslant -2$ or $x \geqslant 2$
b)

17 Indices

1 **a)** a^7 **b)** $4p^6$ **c)** q^4

2 **a)** 16 **b) i)** c^9 **ii)** d^5

3 **a)** -6 **b)** t^4

4 **a)** 20 **b)** $2p^7q^5$ **c)** $48r^2$

5 **a)**

x	-4	-3	-2	-1
y	6	1	(-2)	-3

x	0	1	2
y	(-2)	1	(6)

b)

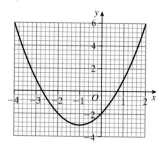

6   **a)** x^3 **b)** y^2
7   **a)** $27a^{12}$ **b)** $2p^3$
8   **a)** 1 **b)** $16p^{12}q^{16}$ **c)** $r^{-6}t^8$
9   **a)** $16x^8$ **b)** $\dfrac{2}{x}$

18 Proportion

1   **a)** $E = 0.25T$ **b)** 2.5
    c) 26 newtons
2   **a) i)** $A = 0.5D^2$ **b)** 84.5
    c) 18 cm
3   **a)** $y = \dfrac{3\sqrt{x}}{2}$ **b)** 3.75
    c) 4096
4   **a)** $M = 0.016r^3$ **b)** 6.75 kg
    c) 50 cm
5   **a) i)** $V = \dfrac{1000}{P}$
    ii)

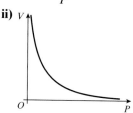

    b) 2 m³
    c) 125 newtons/m²
6   **a)** $d = \dfrac{2.4}{\sqrt{h}}$ **b)** 0.75 **c)** 0.64
7   **a)** $F = \dfrac{32}{D^2}$ **b)** 1.28 **c)** 1.6
8   **a)** $x = 4.9t^2$ **b)** 122.5
    c) $1\frac{1}{7}$ seconds

19 Function notation

1   **a)** 4 **b)** 1.5
2   **a)** $1 - 3x$ **b)** $5 - 3x$
3   $f^{-1} : x \mapsto \dfrac{3}{x} - 2, x \neq 0$
4   $\frac{1}{4}$
5   **a)** -9 **b)** $-1.6, 0.2, 3$ **c)** 3
6   **a)** -9 **b)** 1.5 **c)** 6
    d) $x < -1$
    e) $g^{-1} : x \mapsto x^2 - 1$
7   **a) i)** 2 **ii)** -7 **b)** 1
    c) i) $ff(x) = x$ **ii)** f^{-1} is the
    same as f
8   $x = 1, x = 1\frac{7}{8}$
9   **a) i)** -3 **ii)** -2
    b) $f^{-1} : x \mapsto \dfrac{x + 3}{4}$
    c) i) $gf : x \mapsto \dfrac{4}{4x - 3}$ **ii)** 0.75

20 Harder graphs

1   **a)**

x	-4	-3	-2	-1
y	-19	(-3)	1	-1

x	0	1	2
y	-3	1	17

    b)

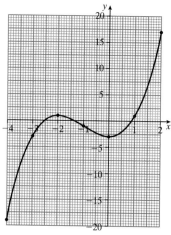

    c) i) $-2.6, -1.3, 0.9$ **ii)** $-2, 1$

2   **a)** $(-1, 7)$ **b)** $1.6, -3.6$
    c) $-3.8, 0.8$
3   **a)**

x	0.4	0.6	0.8	1
y	10.4	(7.3)	5.8	(5)

x	1.5	2	3	4
y	(4.2)	4	(4.3)	5

x	5	6
y	(5.8)	(6.7)

    c) $0.75, 5.2$ **d)** $y = 10 - 2x$
4   **a)** -3 **b)** $-1.9, 0.3, 1.5$
5   124 (accept answers in range
    115 to 135).
6

x	1	2	3	4
y	500	150	93.3	80

x	5	6	7
y	79.2	83.3	89.9

21 Calculus

1   **a)** $8x - 4$ **b)** 0
2   $\dfrac{dy}{dx} = 8x - \dfrac{1}{x^2}; \ (\frac{1}{2}, 3)$
3   $\frac{1}{3}$ m/s²
4   **a)** -2 **b)** $\dfrac{2x}{3} - 4$
5   **a)** $3t^2 + 6t - 9$ **b)** 12 m/s²
6   **a) i)** $6 - 4x$ **ii)** $(1.5, 11.5)$
    b) maximum; eg coefficient
    of x^2 is negative **c)** $x = 1.5$
7   **a) i)** $3x^2 - 6x - 9$
    ii) $x_A = -1, \ x_B = 3$
    b) 13 and -19
8   **b)** $840 - 60x$ **c)** $780
9   **a)** $3x^2 + 75$ **b)** $(2, 58)$ and
    $(-2, -258)$ **c)** none
10 **b)** $8x - \dfrac{216}{x^2}$ **c)** 4 cm

SHAPE, SPACE AND MEASURES

22 Average speed

1   24 km/h
2   76 km/h
3   11.63 s
4   2 hours 24 minutes
5   19.8 km
6   712 km/h
7   3567 km
8   12 hours 25 minutes
9   0.006 m/s
10 16 hours 36 minutes

23 Construction

5   a) 2.1 m   b) 64°
6   420 m (accept answers in range 415 to 430)
7   246 m (accept 240 m to 250 m)
8   a) 220 km   b) 280°

24 Geometry

1   a) $x = 76$ [(vertically) opposite angles; corresponding angles]
    b) $y = 67°$ [sum of angles on a straight line $= 180°$; alternate angles (or corresponding angles)]
2   $\angle PTQ = 69°$ [$\angle PQT = 63°$ (corresponding angles) $\angle PTQ = 180° - (63° + 48°)$ (angle sum of triangle)]
3   43° [alternate angles; (vertically) opposite angles; angle sum of triangle]
4   116° [alternate angles; base angles of an isosceles triangle; angle sum of a triangle]

5   a) 1080°   b) 36°
6   a) 140°   b) 40°
7   a) 12   b) 64°
8   a) 18   b) 2880°
9   15
10 20
11 a) 038°   b) 218°
12 092°

25 Transformations

1   a) Rotation of 90° clockwise about the origin
    b)

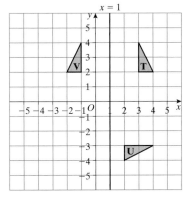

2   a) Reflection in the line $y = x$
    b)

3   a) b)

4   a) b)

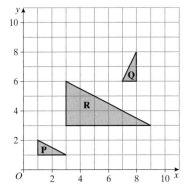

5   a) Translation with vector $\begin{pmatrix} 4 \\ -2 \end{pmatrix}$

    b) i) Enlargement with scale factor 2, centre (2, 0)
    ii) Enlargement with scale factor $\frac{1}{2}$, centre (2,0)

6

7

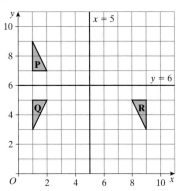

Rotation of 180° about the point (5, 6)

8

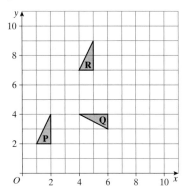

Translation with vector $\begin{pmatrix} 3 \\ 5 \end{pmatrix}$

26 Circle properties

1 29

2 **a)** 33° **b)** A line drawn from the centre of a circle to the midpoint of a chord is perpendicular to the chord. Angle sum of triangle = 180°.

3 28°

4 134°

5 **a) i)** 38° **ii)** Angles in the same segment are equal
b) 52°

6 **a) i)** 61° **ii)** Sum of opposite angles of a cyclic quadrilateral is 180°
b) 29°

7 **a) i)** 148° **ii)** Angle at the centre is twice the angle at the circumference
b) i) 74° **ii)** Angles in the same segment are equal.

8 **a) i)** 39° **ii)** Angle at the centre is twice the angle at the circumference
b) 31° (Sum of opposite angles of a cyclic quadrilateral is 180°.
Angle sum of triangle = 180°. In an isosceles triangle, the angles opposite the equal sides are equal.)

9 **a) i)** 62° **ii)** Alternate segment theorem
b) 118°
c) Alternate angles PTC and BCT are equal

10 **a) i)** 51° **ii)** Alternate segment theorem
b) 137°

11 8 cm

12 10

27 Area and perimeter

1 51 cm²

2 8

3 110 cm²

4 172 cm²

5 80 cm²

6 26.1 cm

7 88.2 cm²

8 3.77 cm

9 54.5 cm²

10 41.1 cm

11 23.2 cm

12 281 cm²

13 20.1 cm²

14 27.2 cm

15 37 000 cm²

28 3-D Shapes – volume and surface area

1 254 cm²

2 **a)** 3600 cm³ **b)** 2040 cm²

3 **a)** 480 cm³ **b)** 440 cm²

4 **a)** 5090 cm³ **b)** 1640 cm²

5 273 cm²

6 **a)** 437 cm² **b)** 860 cm³

7 208 cm²

8 231 cm³

9 2470 cm³

10 **a)** 82.8 cm³ **b)** 127 cm²

11 37.2 cm²

12 149 cm²

13 214 cm²

14 1.36 cm

15 640 000 cm³

29 Pythagoras' theorem

1 7.44 cm

2 2.4

3 6.69

4 8.4 cm

5 9.88 cm

6 22.2 km

7 6.09 cm

8 32.9 cm²

9 17.7 cm²

10 8.06 cm

11 13

12 49.3 cm²

13 **a)** 90° **b)** 9.72 cm

14 7.71 cm

15 10.6 cm

16 23.2 cm

17 132 cm³

18 171 cm²

19 79.8 cm³

20 32.1 cm²

21 27.6 cm

22 8.51 cm

23 11.5

24 7.93 cm

25 44.4 cm²

30 Trigonometry

1 3.47 cm

2 36.7

3   3.64 cm
4   61.6°
5   8.46
6   2.51 cm
7   31.9
8   8.28 cm
9   1.71 m
10 076°
11 293 m
12 19.8 m
13 42.7°
14 10.3 cm
15 21.9 cm
16 3.2°
17 10.7 cm
18 6.27 cm
19 12.5°
20 3.71 cm
21 43.3
22 7.99 cm
23 37.9°
24 7.55 cm
25 6.96 cm

31 Similar shapes

1   a) 76° b) i) 5.4 cm ii) 1.2 cm
2   a) 5.4 cm b) 13.5 cm^2
3   a) 9.1 cm b) 3.6 cm
4   a) 3.9 cm b) 5.4 cm^2
5   a) 25:16 b) 16:9
6   a) 7 cm b) 6.6 cm
7   a) 3.2 cm b) 4.2 cm c) 16:9
8   No; e.g. $\dfrac{110}{100} = 1.1$

    but $\dfrac{90}{80} = 1.125$

9   a) 10.2 cm b) 4.9 cm
    c) 270 cm^2
10 a) 8.1 cm b) 7.6 cm
    c) 48 cm^2
11 a) 352 cm^2 b) 162 cm^3
12 a) 15 cm b) 1750 cm^3
13 a) 18 cm b) 999 cm^2
14 a) 9 cm b) 216 cm^3
15 a) 303 cm^2 b) 4850 cm^2

32 Advanced trigonometry

1   a) 19.2° b) 9.11 cm
2   67.3°
3   69.0 cm^3
4   736 cm^2
5   13.9°
6   a) 16.4 cm^2 b) 6.14 cm
7   7.87 cm
8   42.3°
9   58.2°
10 a) 82.8° b) 22.9 cm^2
11 8.76 cm^2
12 118.5°
13 a) 7.68 cm b) 22.0 cm^2
14 509 m
15 a) 82.1 km b) 095°
16 11.3 cm^2

33 Vectors

1   a) i) $\begin{pmatrix} 3 \\ 5 \end{pmatrix}$ ii) 5.83 b) (10, 11)

2   a) i) $\begin{pmatrix} 2 \\ -1 \end{pmatrix}$ ii) $\begin{pmatrix} 4 \\ -2 \end{pmatrix}$
    iii) AB and CD are parallel.
    $CD = 2AB.$ b) 4.47
3   a) $b - a$ b) $\frac{1}{2}(b - a)$
    c) $\frac{1}{2}a + \frac{1}{2}b$
4   a) i) $4a$ ii) $4a - b$ iii) $a + \frac{3}{4}b$
    b) $\frac{3}{4}$
5   a) $a + \frac{1}{2}b$ b) i) $b + 2a$
    ii) $\overrightarrow{PT} = 2\overrightarrow{PM}$
6   a) i) $a - b$ ii) $\frac{3}{2}a + \frac{1}{2}b$
    b) i) $\frac{3}{2}a$ ii) MN is parallel to
    PQ and $MN = \frac{3}{4}PQ$.
7   a) i) $a - b$ ii) $\frac{2}{3}a + \frac{1}{3}b$
    b) i) $a + \frac{1}{2}b$ ii) $\overrightarrow{PL} = \frac{2}{3}\overrightarrow{PM}$
8   a) $c = b - a$ b) i) $\frac{3}{2}b$
    ii) XY is parallel to UT and
    $XY = \frac{3}{2}UT$
9   a) i) $b - a$ ii) $\frac{3}{4}a + \frac{1}{4}b$
    iii) $a + \frac{1}{3}b$ b) $\overrightarrow{PL} = \frac{3}{4}\overrightarrow{PK}$

10 a) i) $\frac{1}{2}b$ ii) $\frac{1}{2}b$
    b) Opposite sides are
    parallel and equal in length
    i.e. the quadrilateral is a
    parallelogram.

HANDLING DATA

34 Graphical representation of data

1   a) 10 b) 46 d) approx 56
2   b) cumulative frequencies
    are: 20, 115, 180, 190, 195
    c) i) approx 70 ii) approx 45
3   a) 54 b) 8 c) 6
4   a) bar width 25, height 2.2;
    bar width 10, height 1.6
    b) 24; 35
5   a) 48 b) 216
6   12%
7   a) i) 15 ii) 33 b) 22

35 Statistical measures

1   a) 2 years b) 4.2 years
2   a) 0 b) 1.25
3   60
4   a) i) 30 ii) 29.75
    b) i) increase ii) 30 > 29.75
5   a) 12 b) 2, 8, 8
    c) eg 1, 2, 4, 4
6   61%
7   21 years
8   168 cm
9   26
10 a) $0 \leq d < 2$ b) $2 \leq d < 4$
    c) 114 mm
11 a) $100 < d \leq 110$
    b) $\frac{22}{50}$ or $\frac{11}{25}$ c) 97.2 km/h
12 a) approx 18 hours
    b) approx 4 hours
13 a) 45 000
    b) 4, 20, 36, 46, 50, 52
    d) i) approx 43 000
    ii) approx 17 500

14 a) i) 20 years **ii)** 26 years
b) eg The ages of the players in the cricket team are more spread out.

15 a) 9 **b)** eg The girls' marks were higher and less spread out than the boys' marks.

16 a) 15, 110, 155, 170, 180
c) i) approx 36 **ii)** approx 22
d) approx 24

17 a) approx 34 **b)** approx 34

18 a) 60–79 **b)** 58 or 57.5
c) cumulative frequencies 3, 8, 14, 23, 30

36 Probability

1 a) $\frac{75}{100}$ or $\frac{3}{4}$
b) No; if the coin were fair, it would come down heads approximately 50 times.

2 35

3 21

4 18

5 a) 36 **b)** 96

6 a) 0.55 **b)** 0.35

7 a) 0.2 **b)** 0.65 **c)** 12

8 a) 0.24 **b)** 0.56 **c)** No; eg probabilities should be multiplied, not added

9 a) 0.6 **b)** 0.45

10 b) $\frac{2}{15}$ **c)** $\frac{7}{15}$

11 b) $\frac{9}{64}$ **c)** $\frac{30}{64}$ or $\frac{15}{32}$

12 b) 12

13 b) i) $\frac{2}{15}$ **ii)** $\frac{8}{15}$

14 b) $\frac{6}{36}$ or $\frac{1}{6}$ **c)** $\frac{14}{36}$ or $\frac{7}{18}$

15 b) $\frac{11}{12}$

16 a) $\frac{3}{24}$ or $\frac{1}{8}$ **b)** $\frac{11}{24}$

17 a) $\frac{6}{56}$ or $\frac{3}{28}$ **b)** $\frac{26}{56}$ or $\frac{13}{28}$

18 a) 0.16 **b)** 0.33

19 a) $\frac{3}{40}$ **b)** $\frac{17}{40}$

20 a) $\frac{7}{20}$ **b)** $\frac{13}{20}$

21 a) 0.027 **b)** 0.784

22 a) $\frac{3}{190}$ **b)** $\frac{241}{285}$

23 $\frac{6}{216}$ or $\frac{1}{36}$

24 a) 0.32 **b)** 0.53